Umm . . .

A COMPLETE GUIDE TO PUBLIC SPEAKING

Umm . . .

A COMPLETE GUIDE TO PUBLIC SPEAKING

James O'Loghlin

ALLEN&UNWIN

First published in 2006

Copyright © James O'Loghlin 2006

Allen & Unwin
83 Alexander Street
Crows Nest NSW 2065
Australia
Phone: (61 2) 8425 0100
Fax: (61 2) 9906 2218
Email: info@allenandunwin.com
Web: www.allenandunwin.com

National Library of Australia
Cataloguing-in-Publication entry:

O'Loghlin, James.
Umm- : a complete guide to public speaking.
ISBN 978 1 74114 954 8.

ISBN 1 74114 954 1.

1. Public speaking. 2. Oratory. I. Title.

808.51

Cartoons by Matthew Martin
Set in 12/15 pt Bembo by Midland Typesetters, Australia
Printed in Australia by McPherson's Printing Group

10 9 8 7 6 5 4 3 2 1

CONTENTS

PROLOGUE

Imagine this. You are giving a speech. You're standing on a stage looking out at an audience of 100 people. They are staring expectantly at you, wondering whether you are going to entertain or bore them. You feel the pressure. Your hands are shaking. You open your mouth—and nothing happens. You try again and this time some half-choked, hesitant words emerge. You cough. Someone in the audience coughs. You try to control your nerves. Fail. You know you are supposed to talk, so you do, and the words tumble over each other in such a hurry to get out of your mouth that all that emerges is a rushed jumble of sounds that mean nothing, even to you. Your hands are really shaking now. You see the people in front of you disengage, look away, whisper to their neighbours. A man in the front row sighs and starts to doodle. Your face turns red and your heartbeat races. You feel worse than you have ever felt before. You look at the clock on the wall. Your speech has 29 minutes to go.

Now imagine this. You are giving a speech. You are on stage looking out at an audience of 100 people. They are staring expectantly at you, wondering whether you are going to entertain or bore them. You feel the pressure, and revel in it. You are calm and aware, in control of your mind and body. You start talking and your voice is confident and purposeful. You don't look down at notes, but you know exactly what you are saying, why you are saying it and how you are going to say it. You see that your audience is utterly engaged and eager to know what you are going to say next. You draw them in, pose a question, pause and let the silence hang. You look out at them and you know with complete certainty that at that moment the only thing anyone in that room wants to know is what you are going to say next. It feels very good.

I have been in both positions. If you are interested in public speaking, or you find yourself in a situation where you have to speak in public, and you would prefer to experience the second scenario rather than the first, read on.

INTRODUCTION

The purpose of this book is to help eliminate two forms of agony—the agony of listening to a bad speech and the agony of giving one. Each is painful in different ways. Listening to a bad speech brings boredom of such an intense and powerful kind, you feel that if you are unable to somehow stop the speaker from continuing you may find yourself pulling your ears off so the noise can't get in anymore. Giving a bad speech brings such humiliation and embarrassment that, for the rest of your life, if you ever see anyone who you know was in the audience you will immediately want to run away.

All that pain is preventable. In fact, when it's done well, public speaking can be an informative, interesting, funny, uplifting and utterly pleasurable experience for both audience and speaker.

Public speakers are not born. They are made. Someone who is a bad public speaker can become a good public speaker. And a good public speaker can create as much pleasure as a bad one can create pain. Good public speakers can inspire, they can move, they can cause the listener to laugh, cry and give money. Sometimes they can even change a listener's life.

Public speaking isn't just standing up at a wedding or giving a presentation in a lecture theatre. It is what you do every time you talk to a group of people. If there are six people at a staff meeting and you speak, then you are public speaking. A job interview involves public speaking. Most of us will have to do it at some point, so we may as well learn how.

Public speaking is the most basic, direct and powerful way to communicate. If you can stand in the same room as another person, get their attention and talk to them in a way that makes them want to listen, you have the potential to influence them far more than any email, letter, telephone call, text message or television show can. If you can do it well, you can create magic. You can bring a crowd to life, you can have them hanging on your every word, you can make them think, you can make them laugh, you can even make them love you (at least for a little while).

But if you do it badly, your audience will hate you. Nothing can bore more intensely than a bad public speaker. You can stop reading a boring email or a book, you can turn off the television or the radio, and you can walk out of a movie without offending. But when you are listening to a speech you're stuck, and that explains the murderous thoughts that pop into the head of even the most reasonable person when someone is giving a boring speech.

The other reason a bad speech can be so life-sapping is that, in this age of fast cuts, multiple images and short attention spans—in which even at rock concerts the band has to have obscure moving images on a big screen behind them to prevent anyone having time to think about how much their tickets cost—listening to one person doing nothing but speak is a big ask. The main reason I never saw stand-up comedy until I was in my mid-twenties was because I was conditioned to think, 'One guy just standing there talking—how funny can that be?'

To engage an audience simply by talking, with no props, is difficult. It can easily fail. It is also one of our biggest fears. Most people would rather jump out of a plane strapped to a shark while having a dentist pull out their front teeth than speak in public. Why?

Fear of humiliation. We all care what other people think of us, and there are few things that will cause others to think badly of us more rapidly and intensely than boring them with a bad speech. When I'm part of an audience and someone is giving a bad speech, I feel like I'm dying. It makes me angry.

Those feelings would be unfair if the speaker couldn't help it. If the ability to speak in public was something you were either born with or not born with, like height or looks, it would be grossly unjust to dislike those who couldn't do it. It would be like hating someone for being tall.

But public speaking ability isn't like height. It's like playing the violin. Yes, some people are naturally better at it than others when they begin, but all they have is a bit of a head start. What really determines how good a violinist you will become is how much you learn about it, how much you practise, and how committed you are. And, when it comes to performing, how well you control your nerves. Public speaking is the same.

If you have to speak in public or if you want to be able to speak in public, you can learn to do it a lot better than you do it now.

And you should want to.

Why? There are several reasons.

It makes you feel good

It really does. If a speech you give, whether at a wedding or at work, goes well, you will feel great. It's a rush. You have successfully held the attention of, and impressed, lots of people. You have expressed your ideas coherently and logically and perhaps even made your audience laugh and think.

Sure, some say real happiness comes from within, and what other people think of you shouldn't be important—and that's all great if you're spiritually evolved—but most of us need every bit of public praise and reinforcement we can get. Public speaking can provide it.

It builds confidence

Public speaking changed my life. I was a timid, underachieving lawyer with no faith in my ability to do anything until I stumbled upon stand-up comedy. When people started to laugh I realised I had succeeded at something that most people were terrified of. It was the beginning of self-belief.

If public speaking scares you—and then you conquer your fear and do it and become good at it—that's got to be deeply satisfying.

It's powerful

Sometimes you can feel everyone in the room hanging on your every word. You know that all anyone wants to do is listen to *you*. You can feel people listening, you can feel them thinking, and sometimes you can even feel them being persuaded that whatever it is you are saying is the most correct and righteous thing in the whole world.

Being good at public speaking gives you an opportunity to persuade and to be perceived as clever and powerful and smart. That's got to be good.

It's useful

If you need support for something you want to do, then the
ability to deliver your message powerfully and persuasively is very
important. Throughout history, people have been motivated to do
all sorts of weird things purely by the power of public speaking.
During wars, the power of inspirational public speeches has
turned ordinary, timid people like you and me into fearless
fighting machines. I advise using such power for good, of course,
not evil, but if you have an idea and you want to get people
fired up about it, being a good public speaker will be of great
assistance. In pretty much any sort of business presentation, the
ability to formulate and speak your thoughts in a coherent, entertaining and listenable way is a huge advantage.

The audience deserves it

Think back on a bad speech you have heard, remember the pain
it caused you, the way it made you writhe in your chair, the way
it made you fidget and made your brain soundlessly scream
'PLEASE, JUST SHUT UP!' You don't want to inflict that pain
on other people, do you? You don't want your audience to hate
you. Life brings enough pain without you adding to it.

If you talk to 100 people for 20 minutes, that's 2000 person
minutes—which is about 33 hours. You wouldn't want to be
responsible for creating 33 person hours of pain, would you? No.

Then learn how to give a good speech.

one
BEFORE YOU BEGIN

You've been given your assignment. You've been asked to give a speech at a fortieth birthday party, or to give a presentation at work, or to address a sales conference. You know the length of time you have to speak for and you know the topic, but that's it. Maybe you don't even know the topic. You stare up at the computer screen and there, typed very neatly in utterly appropriate font is your speech so far: one word, 'Hello'. The word stares back at you. You stare back at it. You wonder what comes next. Then for a long time nothing at all happens except that your brain starts to implode.

Entertainment

In broad terms there are two types of public speaking. There is the kind whose sole purpose is to entertain—stand-up comedy, for example, and some after-dinner speeches. Then there is the other kind, the majority of speeches, which have another purpose—to toast the bride and groom at a wedding, for example, to inform students about the French Revolution, to explain a new business plan to staff, to pitch for a job or contract, to enlighten people about the pathology of frogs, to thank staff for their hard work over the past year, or to MC a fundraising event as smoothly as possible.

Obviously, the first group of speeches, those whose only purpose is to entertain, must be entertaining to succeed. That's what they're for. But what about the second group? This is one of the most important things I am going to tell you: this second group of speeches must also be entertaining. This is vital. I don't necessarily mean that they must be full of jokes. What I mean is that all speeches must—*must*—make the audience want to keep listening. That is what entertainment is; it's making the audience want to keep looking and listening to find out what happens next. Any good book, film, ballet, television show or sporting fixture does this. Speeches are the same. Entertain the audience; make them want to know what happens next and your other aim—the imparting of certain information—will become immeasurably easier.

This doesn't mean you have to tell lots of jokes, or pretend you're a comedian or juggle or do a handstand. I'm not talking about being funny, but you do need to remember at all times to package and arrange and deliver the information you are trying to impart in such a way as to make the audience want to keep listening to you.

> Giving a speech in which you want to communicate information to the audience is a bit like having sex to get pregnant. Impregnation may be the primary purpose of the act, but it will only really work if everyone involved is enjoying it. If it's not fun, you probably won't achieve the primary aim of getting pregnant. And if your audience doesn't enjoy your speech they're unlikely to remember much of its content.

No matter how vital the information you are delivering to your audience, no matter if it will make them money or save their life, if they are bored by the way in which you deliver that information they will hate listening to you, they will shut their ears and their minds, and you will have failed. Your message will not be communicated effectively unless you have the attention of the audience. If people are looking at their watches, wondering how much longer it will last, or daydreaming about hitting the winning runs for Australia in a cricket match, they may as well not be there. In fact, mentally they're *not* there.

Interest them and entertain them in the way in which you convey your information, and you will succeed. Get their attention and keep it, and they will be yours. If they are interested in what they hear, they will take it in. If they are bored they won't. So make your speech entertaining. This is simply said, of course, but hard to do. However, there are ways.

Why are you speaking?

The first thing you need to do when you are planning a speech is to work out *why* you are speaking. It sounds obvious, but many people never bother to do it. For example, at a corporate function where I was the MC I was told that the managing director of one of the evening's sponsors was going to speak.

'Why?' I asked.

I expected the answer to be something like, 'They're paying a lot for the dinner so they want to tell everyone what a great company they are.'

Instead I got a blank look. 'Well,' said the organiser, 'we just thought he should.'

It turned out the managing director didn't particularly want to speak, but because he thought it was expected, he had agreed. The organisers didn't particularly want him to speak either, but because his company was sponsoring the function they felt they should ask him. Predictably, the speech wasn't really about anything and benefited neither the function nor his company.

In everyday conversation we often say things that don't have much point. We make small talk at barbecues because standing in silence next to someone feels awkward. You can't get away with this in public speaking. Everything you say must have a point. Once you've finished saying stuff that has a point, sit down. You're finished. If you haven't got a really good reason to stand up and make a speech, don't do it.

Each speech should have a clearly defined aim that you can write down in a sentence. If you are doing stand-up comedy your aim is simple—to be funny. If you're giving a toast at a wedding your aim may be to inform everyone about parts of the history of the couple's relationship in a humorous way without offending anyone. If you are giving an address at a conference on mice your aim is to impart some information about mice. If you are speaking at your firm's annual dinner your aim may be to make everyone who works with you realise that you appreciate their efforts, to excite them about the future and, if you are the top dog, to make them feel that you are a fantastic person so they will have warm and fuzzy feelings about their boss. If you are the MC at a fundraising event your aim may be to run the evening as smoothly and amusingly as you can while at the same time persuading everyone there to part with as much cash as possible.

If you have been asked to give a speech, ask those who have asked you why they picked you and what they want the speech to be about. What do they want it to achieve? Hopefully they'll know. If not, you need to work it out with them.

Sometimes the request will be very specific. You may be asked to talk about your field trip to Algeria, or to share your expertise on Senegalese oak trees. When this happens then you know what your talk is about.

Or the request may be general. You may just be asked to educate and inspire the audience. Often when I am asked to speak at corporate functions, I am simply told that the organisers want me to be funny, and for what I say to be relevant to the experiences of the people who will be in the audience. That's enough. I then know the aim of my talk—to be funny and relevant.

Sometimes you won't be told anything helpful. Then you have to work out for yourself what the aim of your talk will be. Firstly, work out how wide the parameters are. If you are talking to a group of people you work with, your talk will need to be relevant to what you all do. If you are talking at a conference on fishing, your talk needs to have something to do with that subject.

Secondly, think about what your area of expertise is within those parameters. What knowledge do you have that others don't? What experience have you had that may be relevant and useful to discuss?

Then think harder. It's not often that you are given the opportunity to say whatever you like to a group of people. It is a privilege. All those people will be listening to you, and if you have been given some freedom and flexibility in deciding what topic you speak on, it's a wonderful opportunity to talk to people about something that you think is important.

So, given the broad parameters of the speech and the basic unifying feature of your audience, write down the most important things you want to say. For example, if you were giving a talk to students at your old school, what would be the most important things you would say to them? Imagine yourself back then. What would you have liked someone to have said to you? Or, if you are the boss and you're talking to people who work for you, write down the most important thing you want to get across to them. When you were sitting where they are, and your boss talked to you, what did you find interesting and inspiring? And what did you find deadly dull?

Next, within the broad area within which your speech must fall, write down some topics. If you have to give a talk on something to do with ageing, for example, write down thirty things that come into your mind about ageing. You might think of things like maturity, responsibility, physical decay, mental decay, helplessness, wisdom, reflection, proximity to death, wrinkles, loneliness and fear. Or you might think of quite different things. If your talk is about your company you might think about profits, retrenchments, morale, the physical environment, technology, work/life balance and innovation.

Then ask yourself:

- Which of these topics are most relevant to the audience?
- Which of them are likely to be of most interest to the audience?
- Which of them do I have most knowledge of?
- Which of them do I have most experience of?
- Which of them am I most interested in?

It may be obvious from your answers which topic or topics you should pick to speak about, but then again it may not be. In particular, you may find that the topics about which you have the most experience and expertise are not the ones you are most interested in. You may be most interested in some new aspect or discovery about your topic that you know little about. There's no right or wrong thing to do in this situation. Just remember that if you pick a subject that you don't know much about, you'll have to do more work than if you pick a subject you are very familiar with.

Perhaps the most important thing is to pick something to talk about that you think matters. If what you are talking about is not important to you, everything that follows—researching, writing and delivering your speech—will be more difficult, and quite possibly pointless.

Don't be afraid if at first the aim of your speech looks really broad and vague. For example, if you are giving a speech at a fortieth birthday party, all you may start with is the aim of saying something entertaining about the birthday person. That's fine. As long as you have an aim, you have something to start with.

Sometimes it will fall to you to give a talk about something you don't find interesting. Don't write a subject off too quickly. If you look hard enough you can find something interesting in practically any subject. To test this theory, on radio I once challenged listeners to come up with the most boring idea they could think of for a radio story. The winner was 'The History of Financial Institutions Duty in Australia 1984–1987'. I had to do a ten-minute story on it the following day. Believe it or not, in my desperation I managed to find enough material about this obscure subject to create an interesting story.

So look hard. And if you can't get interested in the subject you are speaking on, all is not lost—get interested in the fact that you are giving a speech. Approach the talk as a challenging exercise, and test yourself to see if you can make a fascinating speech about a subject you find dull.

Sometimes you may think that the subject you have been lumbered with is one that people cannot help but find boring. Remember, however, that most people are naturally curious about things they know nothing about. Whether they find your presentation fascinating or dull will be more about *how* you impart the information than *what* information there is to impart.

If you are stuck with talking about a subject that bores you, be professional. Act like it matters. Look for things to make it matter, and after a while, who knows, maybe you'll find something that actually is interesting and that you do think matters.

13 questions to ask

There are several things you need to find out before you start writing your speech. It's important to gather as much information as you can about the situation in which you will be speaking and about your audience. And the questions apply whether the occasion is large or small, formal or informal.

Your immediate reaction will probably be to rush right in and start working out what you are going to say, but you will be in a much better position if you first find out as much as possible about the circumstances.

So ask lots of questions. And write down the answers, because you may not get around to writing the speech for a few weeks.

1 What is expected?

It's important to know what those asking you to speak are expecting from you. Why have they asked you? What do they want your speech to achieve? What is the purpose of the whole event? Do they want your speech to be packed full of information the audience can take away and use, or do they want it to offer light relief?

2 How long?

How long do they want you to speak for? Organisers will usually have a time in mind—but treat this as only the starting point for negotiation. Never agree to speak for a time longer than you feel comfortable with. If you think what you have to say will take half an hour and you've been allotted an hour, ask for the time-slot to be shortened. Good public speaking has no padding, no filling, so don't agree to speak for longer than you need.

I would advise anyone against ever agreeing to speak for longer than an hour. Imagine being in the audience. After an hour you've pretty much had enough of anyone. Even if they're telling you the meaning of life, after 60 minutes your concentration goes out the window—then it's all just 'blah blah blah'.

Sometimes it can be good to allow 5 to 15 minutes for questions at the end of a speech, depending on the subject of your talk and the type of function it is given at. Ask yourself if what you are talking about is likely to raise a lot of questions in people's minds. If it's a talk on the future of computers to a bunch of people who work in the computer industry, yes. If it's the treasurer's report for the bowling club then, unless you're in the red, no.

If you've been allocated an hour for your speech, breaking it into a 40-minute talk followed by 20 minutes of questions can work well. Changing the dynamic of what is going on two-thirds of the way through the hour helps to keep the audience interested and involved. During a question and answer session they will hear different voices, have an opportunity to be involved themselves and see you responding in a different way.

Question time, however, only works if people ask questions. There's nothing worse than ending on the big downer of:

And we've got time for some questions, so . . . are there any questions? . . . Any at all? . . . Yes, up the back there . . . Oh, you were just stretching. Right. Okay . . . well if there aren't any questions then . . . none at all? . . . Okay, well I guess I'll finish then.

> If you are going to take questions, getting the first one is always the hardest—because people are shy—so before you begin, it's a good idea to prime a couple of people in the audience to each have a question ready to start things off if necessary.

After-dinner speeches shouldn't run longer than 30 minutes. I've occasionally seen one go a bit longer and still keep people's attention, but even so, if the audience has enjoyed the talk for half an hour, what do you gain by keeping it going for longer? Nothing. And if all has gone well for 30 minutes, and you keep going, it is possible to undo all your good work and find that your audience has beome irritated and impatient for you to finish. (If your audience hasn't enjoyed the first half an hour, it's way too late to win them over by keeping on keeping on.)

Often organisers think more is better. They may want you to speak for 45 minutes, because this way they think they are getting more for their money—or, if they're not paying you, just more. If you suggest that you only want to do 20 minutes they can often be resistant. They may even think you're not up to it. So I usually say something like, 'I can certainly do 45 minutes if you want me to, but in my experience—and I do quite a lot of these—I've found that usually on nights like this people love to have lots of time to talk and socialise and network. And if we give them a sharp, enjoyable 20 to 30 minutes, they will actually be grateful and it will probably serve the evening a whole lot better.' All of which is true.

Timing may need to be adjusted depending on what happens before you speak. If your speech is preceded by a managing director's welcome, a sponsor's speech, three awards, another sponsor's speech and a thank you to old Harry for his years of faithful service, by the time you're on the audience will probably be pretty full up with words.

The more that precedes you the shorter your speech should be. An audience has a fixed capacity for words, like a jug does for water. Once it's full, it's full—doesn't matter who the speaker is.

3 What time will I be on?

This is particularly vital for any evening speech. If you are on after 10 p.m. it's usually going to be tough. People get tired, people get drunk. There will be more background noise, shorter attention spans and more chatter. There may be many reasons why a speech doesn't work, but for audience members there is only one reason—and that is that the speaker was crap. If you are on at 1 a.m. in the dark with no microphone and a television showing nude mud-wrestling above your head, when it goes badly how many audience members will think that, given the circumstances, you actually did as well as you could have been expected to? None. They will all think the reason your speech didn't work was because you were crap. It's your reputation on the line, so it's very important that you get things right.

Audiences don't make allowances for the fact that it's late or they're tired and drunk and it's too hot and their chair is uncomfortable and they can't hear you properly and they can't even see you because there is a pillar in the way. All these things have a huge effect on a speaker's ability to entertain, but audiences don't make allowances for any of them. If you entertained them you were great, if you didn't you were terrible.

If your speech is going to occur around a meal, there is one rule that only fools break. *Don't speak when people are eating.* If you speak when people are eating you will not have anything near their full attention. You will have, at best, about 40 per cent of it. Food is a basic human need. Listening to public speaking isn't. No matter how good a talker you are, the food will win out, even if it's not very nice. And the noise of knives and forks clinking will distract you and your audience.

The clearing of plates is also very distracting. Most speakers I know have a rule that not only will they not speak when anyone is eating, they will also not speak when plates are being cleared, or when anything else apart from subtle drink service is occurring.

And by the way, dessert counts as eating. People are still distracted by the food (in fact, it's the part of the meal I pay most attention to) and spoons clink as loudly as knives and forks.

So if someone asks you to speak during a dinner or lunch, very politely make it clear you are of the view that speaking during meals doesn't work, but you would love to do it between courses or afterwards. If compromise is impossible I would recommend saying 'no', because you will do more damage to your reputation by speaking under such circumstances than by not. No matter how good you are.

Most organisers will agree to accommodate your desire not to speak during meals, as it is utterly reasonable. But on the night, when things are running late, quite often they will ask you to perform during the main course. You have to be tough and keep saying 'no'.

The two best times to speak during a three-course dinner are between entrée and main, and between main and dessert. Before entrée is a bit early; no one is warmed up and there is less of a vibe. After dessert things can get a bit late and boozy. Be aware that a large proportion of dinners for 20 or more people run late.

If you are giving a 20 to 30 minute after-dinner speech, the best time to do it is after the main course. The reason it's called an after-dinner speech is that it's given after dinner, so people aren't hungry and waiting for food. If they're waiting for food, and they know that they're not going to get it until after you have finished speaking, they'll want you to hurry up and finish. If you speak between entrée and main course, and if the entrée is served at 7.45, cleared by 8.20 and you start at 8.30, they won't be eating until 9 p.m., which is pretty late. And you will be the reason they're hungry.

If you're speaking at a breakfast beware of going on too long, as people often have to hurry off to work.

If you are speaking at a conference there are some things to know about time-slots. Generally, an audience will be more focused in the morning than in the afternoon. If, by the time you get to them, they have already spent five hours listening to other people talk, then it's going to be tough. They will be getting pretty close to being full of words. Try to get a time-slot just after a break rather than just before one, because then the audience will be refreshed by the break, not yearning for it to come. Restlessness sets in as you approach lunch, and subconsciously they resent you for keeping them from it.

If your session relies on interaction, questions and feedback, then go as late as you can in the conference. On day one everyone is shy. By the end, they know each other a bit better, feel more comfortable and will be far more willing to participate.

Over the course of a few months I made three pretty much identical speeches to three separate training groups full of people who didn't know each other. I talked to both the first group and the second group on the second evening of their three-day sessions. On the third occasion I spoke on the first evening, just a couple of hours after the group got together. The audience response for the first two speeches was far more enthusiastic than it was for the third, simply because the people in the audience for the first two speeches had been together for two days and felt more relaxed in each others' company. Those in the third audience were still feeling nervous and uncertain about what was going on, and hence were more inhibited.

Try to avoid speaking on the morning after the big conference dinner. Usually half the people won't come and the other half will be wishing they hadn't. No matter how good you are.

If you are speaking at a wedding or a party, try to go first or second. At these functions there are often too many speeches, and they all go a bit too long. By about halfway through, people have had enough. They've got the point. The bride and the groom have done some pretty silly things in their lives but now they've found each other and, heck, ain't they great together. Try to persuade whoever's running the show not to delay the speeches for too long. The later a night goes the more people want to talk and the less they want to listen. If you don't believe me, next time you go to a party stay sober, look and listen.

4 Will someone introduce me?

No matter what sort of speech you're making, it helps to have someone introduce you. Being introduced serves several functions. Firstly, it gives you status. No matter who introduces you and what they say, the very fact that someone is doing it makes people think you must have something important to say. It's a mark of respect to introduce someone, so they will think you deserve it. The alternative is wandering up there on your own and having to explain who you are and what the heck you're doing there. Hardly a powerful way to start. In fact, slightly embarrassing.

Secondly, if an introduction is done right it can actually create a sense of excitement and expectation amongst the audience that will give you a bit of a head start. For example, 'We're very lucky to have our next speaker here, and I'm sure you're going to find his talk fascinating', creates in the audience a sense of expectation, and it gives the speaker status, even though the intro hasn't actually said anything specific. Without making yourself sound too much like a control freak, I would suggest that you make some 'helpful suggestions' about your intro. Most particularly, that it be brief, two or three sentences at most. (I was once introduced with a laborious reading of my two-page CV. It was dull for them and embarrassing for me.) Give the person doing the introduction a couple of facts about yourself that sound the most impressive and relevant to what you're actually talking about.

Thirdly, if someone introduces you, getting the audience's attention becomes their problem rather than your problem.

Finally, being introduced means you don't have to be the one asking people to turn off their mobile phones and turn their chairs around so that they are facing the stage—which means that you can leap straight into a strong beginning.

5 Will the audience be sitting down?

Usually they are, but sometimes, at cocktail parties for example, they aren't. It's harder to get people's attention when they are standing up, and their attention span isn't as long because their legs get tired. On the upside, when people are standing they are usually more tightly packed together than they would be if they were seated, and that helps generate a vibe.

When your audience is standing it is essential that everyone be able to see you. With any more than about 20 people you will definitely need some sort of riser or stage. It doesn't have to be anything particularly special, but it must be large enough to stand on safely, and high enough for the people at the back to see your face.

Always make sure you are speaking from a fixed point. Sometimes people suggest that you give your speech while just sort of wandering about through the audience. This is a terrible idea. Don't do it. No one can see you properly, there are no lights on you, and you'll have your back to half the audience all the time. Every room has one best place to give speeches from. Find it and do it from there.

6 Is it outside?

Beware of outdoor public speaking. The sound is usually terrible, and it's hard to know how you are going because you can't hear the audience reaction. Your words just vanish into the air.

7 Will there be a lectern?

Will you have notes? If you do, you need something to rest them on so you don't look as though you're taking part in a Year 10 debate. Holding notes in your hand looks very messy. The great thing about speaking from a lectern is that no one can see your notes, so they don't register that you are referring to them.

8 What day of the week is it on?

This question is most relevant for evening talks. Saturday night is the easiest for public speakers, Friday the hardest. Why? On Saturday people are generally well rested and have been doing what they want during the day. If they are out they want to enjoy themselves because it's Saturday night, the jewel of the weekend. They have gone to the effort of going out and they want it to be worthwhile. Therefore they will try to make it worthwhile.

On Friday night most people are at the end of the working week and are tired. They often come straight from work, and have perhaps had a few quick drinks. By the time you get to talk it may all be catching up with them, and they could be getting a bit over-tired. Generally, for Friday night audiences it gets late earlier than it does for Saturday night audiences, so adjust your speaking time accordingly.

Friday night and Saturday night audiences are the two rowdiest of the week. There's a feeling that they *have* to enjoy themselves as much as they can because it's the weekend. During the rest of the week audiences are more mellow. This can mean they are a bit harder to warm up, but they are also less judgmental, and willing to give you a bit more time before they write you off as hopeless. On a Tuesday or a Wednesday night people expect less than they do on a Saturday.

9 Am I being paid?

Sometimes when you are asked to make a speech it will be obvious that you won't be paid. Other times it will be equally obvious that you will be paid. Sometimes, though, you'll be in the grey zone where you're not sure if you are expected to speak for free or not. It's awkward talking about money, but you have to do it. If you are not sure whether the organisers are expecting to pay a fee or not, a relatively delicate way of putting it is: 'Is this some-thing that you have a budget for, or were you hoping to get a speaker to do it without a fee?' If they're not expecting to pay, this allows them to escape embarrassment by saying something like, 'We'd love to be able to offer you payment but no, unfortunately we don't have a budget.'

If giving a talk is conditional, on your part, on getting paid, make this clear early on. If you put off asking about money because you feel awkward about it, then when you eventually get round to it and find there isn't any and want to say 'no', organisers may well feel you have led them up the garden path.

If you do turn down a gig because there's no fee it's unlikely to offend. Many of the people who ask you to speak won't have a very clear idea about how it all works either.

A footnote to this: if you want to become good at public speaking, don't get too excited about being paid for it early on in your career. The more speeches you give, paid or unpaid, the better you get at it. All stand-up comedians start off working for free. Only if and when they become good enough are they offered paid work. In my first few years of stand-up comedy I had a rule that I never turned down a gig. There were times when I hated that rule, especially when I drove for an hour and a half just to experience the humiliation of being paid nothing to get heckled off the stage. But I kept to it because I knew that it was from those hard and horrible gigs that I would learn the most.

10 Who are the audience?

Try to get a profile of the audience. How many people will there be? Will there be more men or women? What is the age range? What do they have in common? Why are they there? Is it because they work for the same company, or because they have an interest in the pathology of frogs, or because their kids go to the same school? Have they paid to attend? If so, how much? Are they all from the same suburb, or same city, or from all over the place? Are they city or country dwellers? Rich or poor?

If it's a work-related talk, what range of jobs does the audience cover? Are they all from the one company, in which case you can talk about that company, or from many? If they are all from the one company, are they all employees, or are clients or suppliers there as well? If they are all from the one industry, what different sorts of jobs do they have in it?

The more you find out about them and what they have in common, the easier it will be to connect.

Here's a simple example of why it's important to know as much as you can about the audience. Say you try connecting with them with a little ice-breaker about the fact that it's rained every day for the past week. Hardly inspired, but everyone notices the weather, right, so it's something. Unless some of the people in the audience flew in that morning from some place where it hasn't been raining every day for the past week. Then your ice-breaker, instead of uniting everyone there by describing something they all have in common, actually becomes a comment that divides the audience into two groups: those from here, and those from elsewhere, who will feel excluded by it. That's not the way to connect. (Ice-breakers are important, and I write more about them in chapter 4, page 121.)

It's great to talk about things that connect those in the audience but you need to know as much as you can about your audience to work out what those things are.

11 What will the audience already know about the subject of my talk?

A speech on the 'The Computer: Past, Present and Future' would be presented very differently depending on whether it was being given to an audience of Year 8 students, first-year uni Computer Science students or IT specialists. Try to work out what level of information your audience will have about the subject you are speaking on, and then start speaking at the point where their knowledge ends.

You have to make sure you aren't telling people stuff they already know (because that's boring) but also that you don't assume they have a higher level of knowledge than they actually do (because then they will get lost).

In many cases working out how much knowledge your audience has won't be a problem. If you are giving a speech to a group of telemarketers about the microbiology of the liver, you can safely assume that most won't know much about the subject. So you just start at the beginning and tell the story. But what if you are giving a talk to a group of telemarketers about effective telemarketing? Obviously they will know something about the subject, but presumably not as much as you (or you wouldn't have been invited to speak to them). You don't want to tell them what they already know, but if you assume too high a level of knowledge they might not understand what you are talking about. In cases like this, ask lots of questions about what the audience does and doesn't know before you start writing.

12 What's been happening?

What will the audience have been doing prior to you speaking? All sorts of things can affect an audience's ability and willingness to listen. I once gave a speech for a company, which was supposed to be funny, and I got absolutely no response. Nothing. Usually when that happens you can work out what went wrong, but this time, try as I might, I couldn't. It was only a few days later, when someone told me that immediately before I was on there had been an extremely bitter and unpleasant annual general meeting, that I understood. No one was in the mood to laugh or even to listen to me properly. They were all thinking about the meeting.

13 How well do they know each other?

If the people in your audience know each other well, if they work for a small company for example, the speech can be much more informal. If you want to, you can mention particular people (but see Inside Information on the next page). If people don't know each other you will need to be more general. The more familiar they are with each other, the more relaxed they will be. If you take questions at the end of a speech, they will usually come a lot more readily from a group that know each other than from a group who don't.

That's a lot of nosy questions to ask. But they're worth asking.

Inside information

Some speakers, especially those whose main purpose is to be funny, place great value on eliciting inside information about the particular group they are speaking to. When addressing an organisation they will endeavour to find out some information about a few of the 'characters' who work there, and some details about the habits or peculiarities of some people everyone knows, like the managing director or the receptionist.

I've always found this risky. The information you get is usually based purely on one person's subjective opinion. What he or she thinks about the personalities of others may not be generally shared. Or they may be mistaken as to how generally known the information is. Even if you get something good, if it's not widely known it won't work as an in-joke. If you have been told everyone knows that Bob keeps a golf putter in his office and spends half the day hitting balls, it could make good material. But if in actual fact hardly anyone knows about Bob's golf putter, when you say 'And what about Bob and his golf putter?', expecting everyone to erupt in laughter, there may just be silence as they all think 'What golf putter?'

Even more dangerously, you may find you are being asked to rely on what the person giving you the information thinks 'will be really, really funny'. It's always dangerous to put yourself in a position where you are dependent on someone else to make calls about what is funny and what will work, because if it doesn't work it's you who gets the blame.

Another possible problem with inside information is that material about someone given to you on the basis that everyone, including the subject, will think it hilarious, may actually offend.

Be really careful about taking advice from someone to 'take the piss out of Charlie, it'll be really funny'. Find out a bit more about Charlie and why someone wants to take the piss out of him, and then check that information with someone else.

If you are going to single out and make fun of someone, do it gently. Ask yourself if what you intend to say is likely to embarrass the person or make them (or others) uncomfortable. There are two reasons for doing this. First, common decency; it's not a good thing to cause others pain. Second, more selfishly, if you pick on someone there's a huge risk that you will look nasty, and that will turn an audience off you very quickly.

So treat with the utmost caution the urgings of people who want you to pick on a particular person. Sure, humour and cruelty overlap—is there anything funnier than seeing someone fall over?—but generally there are better and more inclusive ways of being funny. Looking cruel isn't a good way of winning an audience over.

The basic problem with inside information is that you are trying to talk about things you don't know about. You are trying to tell jokes you don't get. The reason you're speaking is to talk about things you know about, not stuff you don't know about. If you are speaking at a wedding or a birthday you may be inundated with stories about all the wacky things Bill used to do back when he was young and silly. There may be some good material there but beware of overdoing the bowerbird approach. Your job isn't just to collect everyone else's funny stories about

Bill. Bill asked you to speak, he didn't ask all those other people, and the reason he asked you was because he wants to hear your own thoughts.

You also need to work out whether any of these 'hilarious' stories about Bill are going to embarrass him (or his mum). More about that later in Humour, page 63.

I have used inside information on occasion, but always cautiously. If you are thinking of using it, have a face-to-face meeting, preferably with more than the one person briefing you, and ask lots of questions about how widely the information you are being given is known, and how it's likely to be interpreted. Then, when you've written the speech, run it by an insider whom you trust to check you haven't crossed the line from hilarity to offence.

More general inside information, however, can be very helpful. For example, if you are talking to a group of financial advisors, it's helpful to know what they all do all day, and what the big issues facing their industry are. Has there been a big development or issue in the industry recently that everyone is talking about? Is the industry going through a boom period, or through tough times? Why? How has the industry changed over the last few years? New technology is changing everything, so how has it affected this industry? What is the image they have of themselves?

If you are getting a briefing on the type of job they do, beware; many industries these days are so heavily steeped in work-related jargon that when someone is explaining to you how it all works you may have to stop them every few seconds to ask what a 'leveraged double buyback' or an 'NLT' is. Don't be afraid of looking stupid, and don't be put off by the jargon. Jargon isn't clever. It's just replacing words everyone understands with words only a few people understand. And it's better to look stupid before your speech than during it.

two
WRITING YOUR SPEECH

You know why you are making the speech, and you have gleaned all the information you can about the circumstances in which you are making it. You now have to work out what you are going to say. You need to write it.

There is no one correct way to write a speech. Some people start at the beginning and write until they get to the end, some make notes of topics, then gradually flesh out each one with detail, some stare at a blank computer screen for hours until, just as they have got to the stage of really hating themselves, they suddenly have a burst of thought.

Eventually you'll work out what works best for you.

Generally, the key work for speeches is done before you give the speech. Good public speaking is not about leaping onto the stage and winging it. Yes, you want to *look* as if you're leaping onto the stage and winging it, but if you plan and write a good speech, it's hard for it to be a disaster when you deliver it. If you don't prepare, it's easy for it to be a disaster.

Research

The first thing you need to do when writing a speech is to familiarise yourself with your subject. Find out as much as you can about it. Usually if you're talking on a subject it's because you know a fair bit about it already, but you can always find out more. And the process of research will focus your mind. If you're talking about the history of Denmark, find out as much as you can about it. If you're talking about your company's new computer software, find out as much as you can about it. If you're making a speech at a wedding, you will know the bride and groom, so write down everything you can think of about them. Write down their characteristics. If the bride is a procrastinator, write down everything you know about her that illustrates that. If the groom is enigmatic, write down everything you know about him that illustrates that characteristic. Then talk to other people who know them and get their impressions.

Researching a subject is more than reading up on it and talking to people. It's also about looking inside your own brain. If you're giving a speech about a particular person, take some time to trawl chronologically through all your memories of them. Write down everything that might be relevant or funny or interesting. Whatever your subject is, do the same. A good first step in writing any speech is to get every bit of information you have written down in one place.

It's like brainstorming. If you apply your mind to the task of finding out more about your subject, you will find your brain racing with all sorts of thoughts about it. That's good. Some of those thoughts will be gold. Any idea can turn out to be a good one; any bit of information may help. You don't know which bits will be useful yet, so write them all down. Don't judge them. Don't try to work out which piece of information is useful or useless, good or bad, right or wrong. Not yet. Just get them all down.

What if you're speaking about a subject that doesn't lend itself to easily definable research? Perhaps you are giving a talk on 'trust' or 'hope' or 'the future'. Start by writing down everything that the subject triggers in your mind. Expand each thought. Free-associate. In what different ways could you look at the subject of trust? Trust between friends, trust between families, trust between employers and employees. Ask yourself lots of questions. Why is trust important? What is a breach of trust? When, if ever, is a breach of trust justified? What are the consequences of a breach of trust? Do we trust governments more or less than we used to? When and where have you given your own trust? To a hitchhiker by picking him up? To a friend by lending her money? To someone who lives in your street whom you know only slightly and who asked to borrow your car to drive to visit her dying grandma? Has your trust ever been betrayed? Have you ever betrayed another's trust? Where would we be if we trusted everyone all the time? Where would we be if we trusted no one, ever? Etcetera. Answer all these questions and you'll be well on the way.

Keep going, keep asking questions of yourself and free-associating, and write everything down, and before you know it you will have five pages of material about trust. Yes—it's disorganised, it's messy, it's unconnected . . . but it's a lot better than a blank page.

If you get stuck, type the word 'trust' into a search engine and see where it takes you.

Research serves two functions. One is that by doing it you accumulate relevant information. The other is that by continuing to feed your brain information on the topic you focus and stimulate it, and as a result it will almost always reward you by coming up with lots of new ideas and insights.

Even if for a while you feel that what you have come up with is nothing of interest, trust that if you stay focused on the topic and give your brain enough information, time and space to think up ideas, it will.

One of the main purposes of any speech is to tell people what you think, so make sure you do think, and record what you are thinking about—and what you feel. Telling people what you feel can be incredibly powerful in a speech, so be aware of how all this material you're coming up with makes you feel, and write that down too.

> Don't just transcribe material. Analyse it. Don't be afraid to go off on tangents and stray from the topic of your speech. Let your mind go, see where it takes you. The time to cut it all back into a neat shape is later.

Another way of getting raw material is to sit down and talk to someone else about your speech. Sometimes when you are working on your own you get stuck. You feel as if you're going around in circles and can't think of anything new. Changing the dynamic and having someone else to bounce ideas off can free you up.

When you give a speech about a particular subject you have to believe that you have something to tell people that they don't already know. To do that you need to be well informed. You don't necessarily need to know more facts about your subject than anyone else present, although that helps, but you need to have thought hard enough about it to have insights and analyses that they won't already have thought of.

Researching your subject thoroughly will bring confidence, and that confidence will carry on into the writing and delivery of your speech. It's hard to fake or bluff knowledge. It's possible, and sometimes you can get away with it, but ideally when you get up to speak you want to feel confident enough about your subject to know that there aren't any holes in your arguments or any questions you can be asked that will stump you. The only way to know that is to invest sufficient time in preparation.

I don't mean weeks. I know, time is scarce. But you'd be surprised how much information you can absorb on a topic in one intense hour. Usually when we're trying to do something we are constantly interrupted and distracted by phone calls, emails, text messages, television, radio, other people and our own wandering minds, and it's easy to forget how productive one intense hour can be. Next time you have a spare hour, pick a subject you know nothing about, for example bees or the Roman Empire or George Washington or the planet Venus. Sit down in front of a computer, close your email, turn off your phone, then ride the Internet without distraction—an hour later you'll be surprised by how much you know about that subject.

Thorough preparation doesn't mean putting your life on hold for weeks. It just means applying some concentrated, distraction-free effort.

Structure

When you're done researching, read through everything you've written a couple of times and write down anything else that sparks off it. What have you got now? A speech? No way. You've got a disorganised mess of information with no structure.

That's okay.

How do you work out which bits come first, followed by which other bits? How does all this information connect to make a coherent story?

Sometimes the structure of a speech will be obvious and logical. If your topic was 'How to build a house', for example, the best structure would probably be chronological. Start with what you do first—dig out the footings—then work through to whatever it is you do last.

But often—usually—the structure of a speech won't be obvious. Or it may seem obvious at first but then, as you think more about it, other ways of doing it may present themselves. If you were speaking on the causes of World War I, you might start off thinking the best structure would be chronological. Start at the beginning, whenever that was, and work your way through to 1914. But you could also do it thematically. You could examine various causes one after another: imperialism, tension over the Balkans, modernisation, industrialisation, etc. Or you could look sequentially at each of the countries involved: Germany, Britain, France, and so on. There are other ways too.

When I write a speech, structure is often, strangely enough, what comes last. If you lock yourself into a structure too early the danger is that it can operate as a straitjacket. I prefer to look for categories and headings and group together all the bits of information and ideas that relate to that category. By categories I mean pieces of your speech—paragraphs or points that you know you want to refer to at some point. For example, if you were giving a speech about bees, as you gather information you may realise there should be a bit about how they evolved, another bit about how they communicate, another bit about their social structure, another bit about how they get food, a bit about how they build hives and a bit about how, with all their skills, it is inevitable that one day they will rule the world.

Keep returning to your idea of what your speech is about. You may find some fascinating snippets of information that you want to include, but you need to connect what you are saying back to the aim of your speech. The occasional diversion is okay, particularly if it includes something funny or enthralling, but you do need to talk about what you have set out to talk about. However, if in the course of researching your chosen topic you find that, in fact, there is far better material for a speech on a slightly different topic, then, as long as the different topic is an appropriate subject for the talk you are giving, don't be afraid to change.

Returning to that brief description of what your speech is about can also help with structuring it. Does what you are speaking about naturally divide into sub-categories? A talk on 'The game of tennis' could break down into categories of 'how tennis was invented', 'history', 'the rules', 'the shots', 'the greats', and 'recent developments'. Some of those categories naturally break down further. For example, 'the shots' breaks down into 'forehand', 'backhand', 'volleys', 'the serve', etcetera . . . A talk on something as esoteric as love can be broken down into different types of love: 'platonic love', 'romantic love', 'infatuation and love', 'friendship and love', 'self-love' and more.

Even if the information you have collated looks like a mess when you've finished your research, keep looking at it and grouping similar bits together—eventually you'll see topics emerge. As you develop those topics the mass of information will slowly change into a series of coherent points. You may begin to get little inklings of how the different points fit together. You might see that that the bit about how the bride and groom met leads beautifully into the stuff about the groom being vague, because they met when he asked her for directions to the very building he was standing outside. Keep looking at your material and connections will appear.

What if they don't?

Then you're not looking hard enough. Get up, go for a walk and let your mind wander. It's amazing how often that helps. Go back to looking at your material, and eventually you'll see connections between various bits.

> Ideally, leave yourself enough time to allow the topic to percolate through your brain for a while. It's almost inevitable that when you immerse yourself in a topic you'll think of things that fit beautifully while you're washing the dishes or walking to the shops or sitting on the bus.

And just because you're looking at structuring and organising now, it doesn't mean that the time for ideas is over. The time for new ideas is never over. In fact, the more familiar you become with the subject matter of your speech, the more likely you are to have new ideas about it. Keep listening to them and recording them. Some of them could be gold.

Telling a story

You have all the information you need, and perhaps some idea of a structure. What's next? How do you organise a mixture of fact, opinion, analysis and anecdote into a coherent form? What you need to do is transform this jumble of stuff into a story.

A good speech does what a good book, movie or television show does. It tells a story. A story with a beginning, a middle and an end. And a story that has what good stories usually have: excitement, tension, humour, mystery, uncertainty and a resolution.

People have been telling stories since they could talk, and we all like to hear them. The first stories were communicated orally. They were speeches. If you've ever told a story that has held someone's attention, whether it be your child or a couple of friends, whether it was something real or made up, whether it was something funny or exciting or weird or silly or unusual, then you have delivered a good speech.

Once you think of your speech not purely as the transfer of information but as storytelling, then making it something people will want to listen to suddenly becomes easier.

You may think the subject you are speaking on is one that people will inevitably find boring, but whether they find your presentation fascinating or dull is much more about *how* you impart the information than about the information itself.

What a good story always does is to make the audience want to know what happens next. It is the desire to know what happens next that makes you turn the page of a book, that stops you from flicking channels on the television. To make a good speech you have to do the same thing. You have to make your audience want to find out what happens next. If you can do that, your listeners will absorb everything you say.

> By 'telling a story' I don't mean that you should make up stuff. What I mean is that you should arrange the material you have and the information you want to convey in as interesting a way as possible.

This sounds great in principle, but if your topic is 'The migratory habits of the North American mountain goat' or 'A vision for our company's business plan for the next financial year', how do you craft a speech that will make people want to know what happens next instead of counting down the seconds until it's over?

When your subject matter is relatively dry, of course making the audience want to know what happens next is more difficult than when you are telling the story of *Star Wars*, *Alice in Wonderland* or *The Lord of the Rings*. But it can be done. Any information that you need to impart in a speech can be ordered and delivered in an infinite number of ways. One of those ways is the dullest way possible. Another one of them is the 28th most interesting way. Yet another is the most interesting way possible. That's the one we are looking for.

Someone could talk on the subject that interests you most in the world and bore you senseless, and someone else could talk on a subject you find incredibly dull and fascinate you. It's all in the way it's done.

A good speech will never give the audience the impression that its primary goal is to impart information. Rather, it will make the audience feel that they want you to keep talking to find out what happens next. As a by-product of their interest they will absorb the information you are giving them.

You've gathered the information for your speech, you've got all your information and thoughts and analysis down in the one spot and grouped together under loose headings. To turn it into a story, begin by writing down all the information you think is essential. To help you work this out, return to the aim of your speech and start from there. If you were giving a speech on 'The court system in Australia', your speech would need to contain information about the range of different courts in Australia, the different powers each one has, the cases each one hears, and the day-to-day running procedures of each— and, of course, what you have to wear to appear in each one. If your aim was to persuade people to give money to aid cancer research at a fundraising dinner, your speech would need to tell them how people's lives could be improved if a cure for cancer was found, and how their donations could help in finding a cure.

If your speech on Australian courts simply went through the basic information above you would have succeeded in telling people what you were supposed to tell them, but you may well have failed the real test of communication in that you have probably failed to make the audience listen to and absorb what you were saying.

> Think of the basic information your speech needs to convey as a pizza base. It's what the pizza is all about—without it there would be no pizza—but it's pretty plain and dull on its own. It needs a bit of jazzing up to be edible and enjoyable.

The first step in arranging what you want to say in a way that will make people want to listen is to dig deeper. Once you have researched in an information-gathering way, go back and think about it in a totally different way, trying to identify things that would make people want to listen. In other words, having found the ingredients to make the base, now go looking for the topping.

Instead of looking for the facts, look for the stories. Using the example of a speech about the court system in Australia, you might find out what the first case ever heard in an Australian court was. Maybe it was about a swaggie caught sheep rustling or about a soldier who assaulted a botanist who was having an affair with his wife. Or it could have been about a woman trafficking in black market rum. The point is, it may be a story that will bring to life the information you are trying to convey. Look for other interesting titbits. You may find out that the first Australian courthouse was a converted brothel (not true) or that the first chief justice of the High Court was a former premier of Queensland (true).

This sort of information adds flavour to what you are saying. It makes it interesting, but it does more than that. It makes what you are saying memorable. Detail about the first case ever tried in an Australian court is not necessarily information which your audience *need* to know to understand the Australian court system, but it brings what you are saying to life.

Often you will need to explain concepts, such as how the Australian court system works, in a theoretical way, but people always understand theory better if you engage their imagination and give them something they can see in their mind's eye. If you tell them about the first court case involving a sheep rustler, they will see, via their imagination, the court house, they will see the sheep rustler, and these things will help them understand and remember. It will also make them want to know what happens next. If you can paint a word picture so that they see the sheep rustler going into the building that houses the first court in Australia, and see the man who has been given the responsibility of deciding his fate, they'll be thinking, 'Tell me what happens next! Did the guy get convicted? Did the judge get it right? Was the rustler fined a pound or sentenced to death? What happened?'

And if you've got them thinking that, you've succeeded.

Imagine a sporting hero being asked to share the things he has learnt from his career. Here are three ways he could talk about his life:

- He could talk about the way he approached his sport, and what he learnt from doing it:
  I always tried to do my best and I found that if I had done my best, whether I had won or lost, I would be satisfied.

Now there may be a lot in this as a life lesson, but yawn, it's dull.

- He could talk about his experiences:

  There I was at the final bend of the 1500 metres, running 3 metres behind the leader, and I felt I had nothing left. But I reached deep and pushed through the pain and I won.

  An interesting story, but that's all it is. If all he does is share experiences, he hasn't fulfilled the aim of the speech. He hasn't told us what he's learnt.

- Or he could combine experience and analysis:

  There I was at the final bend of the 1500 metres, running 3 metres behind the leader, and I felt I had nothing left. But I reached deep and pushed through the pain and I won. I always tried to do my best and I found that if I had done my best whether I had won or lost, I would be satisfied. And I promise you this is the truth, on that day I felt more satisfaction that I had pushed myself harder than I ever knew I could, than I did about the fact that I had won.

  Here, experience and analysis combine to produce a well-rounded story.

Even though the aim of the sporting hero's speech was to share the life lessons he had learnt, if he had *just* done that it would have been colourless and dull. All base, no topping. By adding the personal experience, the story, the talk becomes far more interesting.

If you can engage your audience's imagination so that they use your words to create pictures in their minds, suddenly they change from passive receivers of information to being your collaborators. You are supplying the words, and they are fitting mental pictures to it. They are involved, they have some ownership of the story.

In the above example, rather than just listening to a host of life lessons, suddenly they are on the track, 3 metres behind the leader at the final bend. 'What's going to happen?' they wonder. Having been involved, they are far more willing to accept a life lesson at the end of the story.

Look out for little nuggets of information that will grab the listener and demand to be remembered, something that next day they will want to tell their friends.

While you're gathering information, look for things that make you go 'gosh'. Something that makes you go 'gosh' will probably make others go 'gosh' too, and then you've got their attention. Look for bits of information or little stories that have what good stories have always had—drama, suspense, humour, ridiculousness, excitement, romance—or anything else that has the 'gosh' factor.

Obviously a talk on the opportunities presented by changes to offshore investment regulation isn't going to have as many 'gosh' moments as the story of the first man in space, but that's okay. You don't need material that could form the basis of an award-winning movie, just stuff that adds a bit of zest and interest, and which increases the average level of excitement and listenability. If you think your talk sounds quite dull and dry, you only have to find something moderately interesting to make it sound less dull and dry.

The other benefit of talking about things that allow listeners to form mental pictures is that it helps them to remember what you are saying. There is a limit to how many words you can remember, but our minds are great at remembering images. If you want to test this, do this exercise with another person. You pick a word—any word—and tell him what it is. Your friend repeats your word and adds one of his own. Then you say your first word, his first word and add another word. Then he says the first three words and adds a word. For example:

Person 1: 'Dog.'
Person 2: 'Dog tomato.'
Person 1: 'Dog tomato happy.'
Person 2: 'Dog tomato happy built.'

Keep going, adding words one after another, and see how long the list gets before you start making mistakes—forgetting words or getting them in the wrong order.

Then do it again, but this time creating a picture in your mind each time a word is added. If 'dog' is your first word, picture a dog. As the second and subsequent words are added, add another picture. You may picture a dog, then a tomato at its feet, then you see the tomato has a happy face, then next to it a wall is being built. I bet you can remember a heck of a lot more words using the second method.

The point is that if you can create visual images you will engage the audience and make them collaborators in the story you are telling them. If you do that they will remember what you say.

Pretty much anything you say that has any theoretical complexity should be illustrated by way of a concrete example. Whether you're talking about saving water, playing cricket, the economy, or the organisation you work for, you need examples. Again, it's about painting pictures and engaging the imagination of the audience.

It's fine for the CEO of a company to say:

> *This company is only as good as its people and I am continually impressed by your devotion and commitment. Thank you.*

But it's a lot better to say:

I had to pick something up from the office last Sunday and when I got here I saw Mary. I asked her why she was in on a Sunday and she said she'd noticed how much everyone likes the plants we have in the office, but that some of them were wilting. She said she'd decided to come in and water them on Sundays. It's a little thing but it speaks volumes about her attitude, and it's typical of the attitude I see from so many of you. Thank you.

If you were giving a speech about 'Love' you could say:

Love is a powerful force.

Or you could say:

Once there was a man who seemed to have everything life could offer. He was rich, he had a wife and three beautiful children, a stimulating job, a lovely house and good friends. One day he decided to leave it all and travel halfway around the world to be with a woman he had spent a total of six hours with. Why? Because he was in love with her. Love is a powerful force.

In both these examples the first option is just words, bald statements backed by nothing. The second option is real, a statement backed up by evidence. It means more. Everyone who hears the story about Mary, whether they know Mary or not, will imagine her driving into the office on her day off to water the plants. They might think Mary is a little bit sad, but the point that the company has dedicated staff will have been made. Everyone who hears the story of the man in love will imagine how strong the feeling must have been to motivate him to leave everything. They might even think about times they have had a similar feeling. The speaker will have got the audience right where she wants them.

Think about ways you can give examples to illustrate the points you are making.

To recap, in planning a speech:

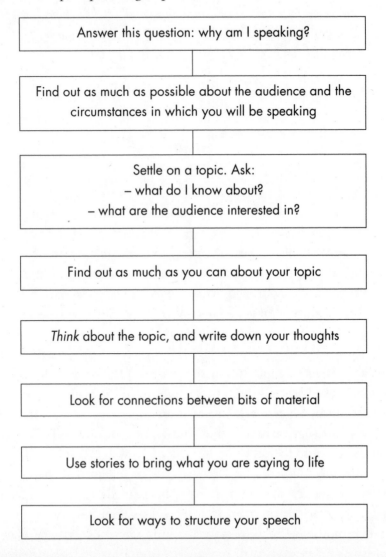

Answer this question: why am I speaking?

Find out as much as possible about the audience and the circumstances in which you will be speaking

Settle on a topic. Ask:
– what do I know about?
– what are the audience interested in?

Find out as much as you can about your topic

Think about the topic, and write down your thoughts

Look for connections between bits of material

Use stories to bring what you are saying to life

Look for ways to structure your speech

It's all about them

Of course we all care about the big wide world and all its joys and problems, but what the majority of us care about most is ourselves and our own little world. Whatever's on the front page of the newspaper this morning, few of us will care more about it than about having to stay late at work to finish something, or about whether our daughter's cold will get better.

A very effective way of making your audience care about what you are saying is to make it about them. One simple way of doing this is to ensure the story you tell is not one where they are merely passive observers, but one where they feel as though they are active participants.

Here are three different ways you could tell people about the role of oil in a car engine. Which do you think is the most effective?

1. Oil acts as a lubricant by forming a layer between metal engine surfaces.

2. If a person complains to a mechanic that their engine has seized, one of the first things the mechanic might check is whether the engine has enough oil. Oil acts as a lubricant by forming a layer between metal engine surfaces and if there is no oil in an engine, then it can't work.

3. Imagine you're driving along a highway at 100 kilometres an hour. You come to a bend and as you turn the wheel, the steering seizes. You slam on the brakes and skid out of control, spinning round and round, just missing other cars and eventually sliding off the road into some bushes. Your heart's thumping but somehow you are okay. What the hell happened? Your car ran out of oil, that's what. Oil acts as a lubricant by forming a layer between metal engine surfaces and if you don't have enough of it, your engine won't work.

Which is better?

1. It's just facts. To remember it is a chore.
2. Better. You have an image of a car being brought to a mechanic, but there are no stakes. Nothing in that story really matters. It's just another story about a car with a problem. There's no real reason to remember it.
3. Best. You—the listener—are a participant in the story. You are in danger and you imagine yourself in that car. There is a mystery. Why did the steering lock? You want to know the answer. So when you are told the answer—that the car didn't have oil—you remember it. And the next thing you want to know (if you didn't know already) is how running out of oil can cause you to end up in such danger. So when the explanation of what oil does in a car comes, you listen and remember. It will stick because the speaker has connected the terrifying image of being in an out-of-control car spinning off the road to the idea of running out of oil.

As much as possible, give a speech where the story you tell involves things happening to the listener. Try this. Once you've written out the dry facts of your speech, go through and after every paragraph write the words, 'Imagine if you . . .'. Then finish the sentence, illustrating the theoretical knowledge you have described with a real example where the listener is the protagonist.

If you were talking about the French Revolution in 1789, these are at least two of the ways you could put the listener in the story:

Imagine if you were a poor worker in Paris and suddenly people were telling you that there was no good reason why the King should take your money by taxation and live in luxury. How would you feel? And how would you feel if they said it was possible to create a different world, one where you didn't have to bow and scrape to anyone. And if they said that to create that world you had to fight, would you?

Or:

Imagine you were the King of France and your family had ruled the country for generations. Suddenly thousands of people were outside your palace screaming for you to be killed. Imagine them screaming for your blood. How would you feel?

If you can put the listener in the story, you will bring your talk to life. It is possible to do this with even the dullest bits of information. For example you could say:

If your computer has a total system failure, there is a blue button on the back of the computer and when you push it it will automatically save your last five days' work to a CD.

But it would be far more powerful to say:

Imagine you have been working day and night on a project for the last five days, and an hour before the deadline your computer has a total system failure. Imagine how you'd feel. It's okay. Don't panic. There's a blue button on the back on the computer. Just push it and your last five days' work will automatically be saved to a CD.

Adopting this technique isn't just some gimmicky trick. If you can get people to imagine themselves in a situation with real stakes, they are far more likely to remember whatever it is that you want them to remember. In this case they will connect the idea of a massive computer crisis with that blue button, so that when they do have a massive computer crisis, they'll know what to do.

Another example: You want to tell some salespeople how to sell your company's new telephone. You could say:

> It is important to emphasise the high-tech features of the new model. Ensure the customer is aware that the new phone contains a video camera and a hair dryer.

Or you could say:

> And you can say to the customer, 'And by the way, madam, if you buy this phone your electricity bills will be a lot lower' and when she asks you 'Why?', you can say, 'Because you can chuck away your hair dryer . . . And you won't have to buy a video camera either.'

The first method is pure theory, whereas in the second the listener has a picture of themselves in the story talking to a customer. It's vivid. It's more real. It means more. And even if they think that what you are telling them to say to the customer is crap, they will still be involved. They will be working out what they can say that will work better.

Make it matter

The best speakers relate what they say back to the lives of the people in the audience. Their listeners leave the room thinking they have found out something that they can use to make their lives a little bit better in some way. You need to look for ways to connect whatever it is you are talking about to the lives of those listening to you.

One way is to invoke a sense of a shared challenge. Ask yourself what challenge the people in your audience share, then work out how you can say something that will help them meet that challenge.

For example, a group of salespeople will all face the challenge of selling more of whatever it is they sell, so tell them something that helps them do that. A group of lawyers all face the challenge of being lawyers. What does that mean? It means they have to deal with people who have some sort of legal problem, and therefore who are probably stressed. The lawyer has to work out how to solve each problem in the best way possible, they have to work in an adversarial environment with the lawyers on the other side, and they have to present cases in court. So give them some information in your talk that will help them meet at least one of those challenges.

Keep reminding the audience why what you are saying matters. If you were talking about the French Revolution it would be easy for your speech to be interesting but not important. That is, people would walk away thinking, 'Gee, that was fascinating. I didn't know about all that; I guess it would have been pretty scary to be the King, but I have to get back to the real world now.' If that's all they are thinking, your speech has not been fully successful. You need to connect with your audience's own lives. In speaking about the French Revolution, you could say:

> *When I think of those peasants armed only with pitch-forks, taking on the heavily-armed French army because they wanted to create a fairer world, I think about the challenges in my own life, and whether I am courageous in facing them.*

Or you could say:

> *When I think about the King in his palace, suddenly terrified, after years of luxury, of being killed by the mob, it makes me realise that none of us can take anything for granted. Everything we see as permanent could vanish. Which is scary, but it also makes me want to make of the most of everything while I can.*

In both these suggestions you are discussing how you are affected, not how your audience should be affected. The implication, however, is obvious: that those in the audience can also, if they want to, reflect on how the material in your speech is relevant to their own lives. If you tell your audience how they should feel, you will sound too didactic, as if you are telling them what to think. This is a didactic way of putting it:

> *Think about those peasants armed only with pitchforks, taking on the heavily-armed French army because they believed in creating a fairer world, and then think about the challenges in your own life, and how courageous you are in facing them. When you think about them, those peasants should make you want to be more courageous.*

Being told what to think immediately makes me resist. It is great to lead the horse to water; that is, to suggest possible lines of thought to your audience. But it is counterproductive to go further and tell them the conclusions they should reach.

Don't be afraid to grapple with the big questions. I don't mean that you should make your speech a philosophical lecture about existence, but no matter what the subject of your talk, surely you can find something to say in it that at least gives members of the audience something to think about as they try to work out how the heck to live their lives.

Say you were giving a speech on how to change a car tyre. Would it be possible to incorporate some information that will help people to answer the challenge of living their life as best they can? Yes. In fact, the only reason they are there in the first place, listening to you, is that they believe learning how to change a car tyre will somehow improve their life. Merely by telling them how to do it you have helped them. But then you can add icing:

> *Learning to change a car tyre isn't going to change your world, but what it might do is make you feel a little more in control when you're in the car, and a little less anxious about being the victim of an unpredictable event, such as a flat tyre, that will leave you helpless. It's not a bad thing to be self-reliant, and learning this simple skill will make you a little bit more so.*

What if you are talking about something far more esoteric, such as the feeding habits of the North American mountain goat? What possible point of connection could that subject have with your life or your audience's lives? Well, I bet that if you found out enough about those mountain goats and their feeding habits, and thought hard enough about it, you would be able to find something that illustrated tenacity, or adaptability, or flexibility, or interdependence, or something else that would be relevant to how you and I live our lives.

I'm not saying that every speech should contain a trite little fairytale lesson, but if you can connect what you are saying in some way to your listeners' lives, to their hopes, their dreams, their fears, their loves, their hates, their jealousies or their something elses, they will take more notice of you.

Ultimately most people are more interested in people than they are in things, so try to put something about people in your speech. You can do this in three ways. You can talk about the people who appear in your speech; you can talk about your own reaction or relationship to that which you are talking about; or you can talk about the members of your audience.

Imagine you were talking about the first man in space. Firstly, you could tell the story of his stepping out into a place that every human being for tens of thousands of years had looked at, but none had ever been to.

Then you could talk about how it affected you. For example:

> When I first heard that story, I knew that if it had been me I would have been terrified, but imagine how exciting it must have been to be the first person ever to step out into outer space where no one had ever been before. I decided then that I wanted to live a life of adventure, too. And so the next day I quit my job at the bank.

Or:

> And I realised that all the time and money and effort that had gone into the space race culminated in this. One man in space and then he came home again. And I wondered why all that time and money and effort hadn't gone into feeding the starving. And the next day I resolved to work even harder at the bank and get as many salary raises as I could, and that I would give ten per cent of my money to charity (or something else).

Then you could take it one step further and talk about how the story might affect those in the audience. For example:

And I wonder if you feel that there's been enough adventure in your life. Maybe there has been, I don't know. But perhaps on the way home tonight you might want to have a think about whether when you get toward the end of your time you might think you went a bit long on safety and a bit short on adventure. And if you do think that, well, it's up to you of course, but maybe you should do something about it.

Or:

And I wonder if in your life you've got your own personal space race. Not a real one, but something you pour a lot of money into, but when it really comes down to it, it's not something you really need and it's not something you get a lot of joy from. Have a think about it and if there is, maybe there's a better way of spending the money.

The above sequence involves firstly telling a story about a third party and then distilling something from that story that affected you. Finally, you ask the audience to consider reflecting on the story in the same way.

It's great if you can give the audience something to think about on the bus home. Because often they will.

Note how careful I was, in speaking of changing a tyre and of the first man in space, to avoid telling people what to think. If you bluntly tell people that they haven't got enough excitement in their lives, or that they should give more money to charity, you will probably put them offside. If you want to persuade people, lead them gently to the area in which you want them to think, invite them to reflect and leave them alone. Some will come to agree with you, some won't. But if you tell people what to do, all you will do is irritate them.

Give your listeners all the facts, and invite them to form their own conclusions. If you've made a good case, be confident enough to allow the members of your audience to make up their own minds. If your listeners are grown-ups, treat them as such. Don't try to tell people what they are feeling or why something is important to them. Don't tell them what conclusion to reach. You can tell them that *you* think what you are about to say is important, and you can tell them what *you* are feeling and why it's important to you. Do this with honesty and commitment, and trust that it will connect. Make your case, lead the horse to water, but resist the temptation to apply pressure to the back of its neck. All that will do is give the horse a good reason to run away.

As you shape your talk keep asking yourself two questions: 'How does this affect me?' and 'How does this affect the people listening?' Keep returning to those two questions, keep trying to answer them, and you'll be on the right track.

Talking about yourself

A good speech must have relevance for those listening to it. That doesn't mean you can't talk about yourself. In fact, many great speakers, on the face of it, do nothing other than talk about themselves. But what they also do is bring the audience with them, so that those listening feel they identify with the speaker, that they understand and empathise with the speaker. It's like when you read a book or go to a movie and see the story through the central character's eyes. If it's done well, you feel the hero's problems and triumphs as if they were your own, his world becomes your world.

However, people can also talk about themselves and be utterly boring. How many times have you found yourself stuck listening to people who just rattle off endless stories about themselves, to the point where you were forced to pretend you needed to go to the toilet to escape?

What is the difference between speakers who talk about themselves in a way that is entrancing and speakers who talk about themselves in a way that is boring?

People who bore you senseless while telling you stories about themselves are usually, whether they know it or not, talking with the intent of impressing the listener. They are thinking (often subconsciously) that if they tell a few stories about what winners and legends and heroes they are, everyone will think they are winners and legends and heroes. Unfortunately the opposite usually occurs. You end up thinking they are egotistical. But if you tell a story where you don't try to bignote yourself, in which you show modesty and humility and, most importantly, allow the audience to relate to you as a normal everyday person, people will relate to you more. Here are two ways you could tell the same story. First version:

> I was on this bus and a little old lady got on, and I really believe that you should be courteous to old people because that's the right thing to do, so I immediately offered her my seat, and she was very grateful. So I helped her sit down, and then as I was standing up, the bus hit this enormous pothole—it must have been huge—and someone bashed into me and pushed me over. And all these people laughed, which I thought was unnecessary and immature. Then the old lady stood up and said to me, 'Excuse me, would you like my seat?' and everyone laughed even more. Honestly, after I'd been nice to her and given her my seat, she just made fun of me, I couldn't believe it.

What's going on here? The speaker is taking a potentially funny anecdote and killing it because his ego makes him take it all too seriously. Have a look at the message behind each sentence of that story:

Sentence 1: I was on this bus and a little old lady got on, and I really believe that you should be courteous to old people because that's the right thing to do, so I immediately offered her my seat, and she was very grateful.
Message: I am a good person because I do the right thing.

Sentence 2: So I helped her sit down, and then as I was standing up, the bus hit this enormous pothole—it must have been huge—and someone bashed into me and pushed me over.
Message: I fell over but it wasn't my fault. I'm not clumsy, I'm a victim.

Sentence 3: And all these people laughed, which I thought was unnecessary and immature.
Message: I can't see the funny side in things when they happen to me.

Sentence 4: Then the old lady stood up and said, 'Excuse me, would you like my seat?' and everyone laughed even more.
Message: I can't see the funny side in things when they happen to me.

Sentence 5: Honestly, after I'd been nice to her and given her my seat, she just made fun of me, I couldn't believe it.
Message: I am so insecure that I need to retreat into pomposity.

Here's another way you could tell the same story.

I was on this bus and a little old lady got on, and I looked the other way and hoped someone else would get up because I was really comfy, then as I stole a look back to see if anyone had, there she was staring right at me and what can you do? So I got up smiling politely while inside I was swearing. So then I was standing up, and telling myself what a good guy I was, when the bus hit this bump or something and I lost my balance completely and sprawled head first onto the ground. Everyone was laughing and I felt like such an idiot. Then the old lady stood up and said, 'Excuse me, would you like my seat?', which was a pretty good line really, and everyone just kept laughing at me.

What's the message behind each sentence?

Sentence 1: Like everyone, I'm selfish, but I also want people to think I'm nice.
Sentence 2: Ditto.
Sentence 3: I fell over because I'm clumsy.
Sentence 4: Like everyone, there are times when I feel like an idiot.
Sentence 5: Even though everyone was laughing at me, I can still see the funny side of it.

By not building himself up as a hero and by allowing his human frailties to show, the speaker builds a bridge to his audience. They think, 'Yes, that could easily have been me. I understand. I'm with him. I often feel stupid too.'

It's not what you say, it's how you say it. You need to be able to see how a listener will perceive what you say. If you are talking about yourself ask yourself these questions: Am I building myself up as a hero? Am I telling people how good I am?

People will relate to what you say far better if you show them your weaknesses, your doubts, your fears and your failings, particularly if at the end of it all you come out okay. We all have weaknesses, fears, doubts and failings, and being able to share is a sign of self-confidence and self-assurance.

This doesn't mean you can't talk about your achievements. Sportspeople, business leaders and celebrities of all kinds are in great demand as public speakers—and people want to hear about their achievements. But they also want to hear the stories behind those achievements. They want to hear about the difficulties experienced on the road to success for two reasons. One, because they too have problems, they have fears, they have insecurities, and if they hear that a world swimming champion experienced those things too, and still managed to succeed, it gives them hope. Two, it makes a better story. Which of these do you think is a better story?

- *I became the fastest swimmer in the world because I am a great athlete and I practised hard.*
- *Despite years of self-doubt and constant injury that frequently drove me to the brink of despair and early retirement, eventually I overcame my fear, made my body strong, found self-belief and became the fastest swimmer in the world.*

The second one, right? Expose your weaknesses and your audience will relate to you. Be human. People are far more interested in what it is like to be human than they are in what it is like to swim fast. If all you do is to tell them that you could always swim fast and how great it is to be able to swim fast, your audience will have learnt nothing they can apply to their own life (unless they too want to be able to swim really fast, and, frankly, not many of us do). But if you tell them about the human experience of becoming the fastest swimmer in the world, and of your own struggle to do so, they will have learnt something of far more depth, and with much wider application. They will be able to take things away from your story and apply them to their own challenges. As they trudge unwillingly to work on a cold morning they aren't going to remember your telling them the importance of a high elbow lift when racing; but they might remember your telling them that if you persevere, with commitment and courage, it will eventually pay off.

> Your speech is not about you. It's about the people listening to it. Even if you are telling the story of your life, it's all about the audience. The most important question you need to ask yourself in public speaking is this: 'Is my speech connecting with the audience?' If it is, then it's a good speech, and if it's not, then it's a bad speech. Whatever you are talking about needs to have some relevance to the audience.

Keep telling them how what you say is relevant to them. I make sure I use the word 'you' a lot in speeches. Listeners' ears prick up when the speaker is talking about them.

If you are telling a story about the time you were in India surrounded by five tigers, you need to bring the audience into that situation. Either explicitly or implicitly, you need to ask, 'How would you feel if you were in the jungle surrounded by five tigers. It would be terrifying, wouldn't it? Well, guess what. It happened to me. So listen up.'

You do that by painting a picture and putting them in it. For example:

> *I was creeping through the jungle when I saw a tiger in front of me. Then I heard a noise to my left. There was*

*another tiger. And another. Then there was a roar behind
me. I turned around and there two more tigers! I was
surrounded by five tigers! Can you imagine being
surrounded by five tigers? Can you imagine how scared
I was? I was terrified.*

Let them know that your reaction to the situation was the normal
human reaction, so that you make it easy for them to imagine
themselves in your shoes—'I was terrified'. To have said, 'Being an
experienced bushman, I wasn't scared at all', would have had a
very different effect. No one could have imagined themselves
in the speaker's shoes because he had signalled that he was not
like them.

The most powerful story in the world is that of the ordinary
person facing extraordinary circumstances. It's *Star Wars*, *To Kill a
Mockingbird*, *Lord of the Rings*, and *Love Story*. The story of a person
surrounded by five tigers is not really about the jungle, or about
tigers. Realistically, no one in the audience is ever going to be
surrounded by five tigers. The story is about overcoming fear, and
reacting well under pressure in a situation with high stakes. These
are things everyone needs to learn to do.

People may walk away saying, 'Wasn't that story about the
tigers amazing?', but they probably won't analyse why. They
would have found it amazing not because it taught them what to
do if they found themselves surrounded by five tigers, but
because they were taken to a place where fear ruled, and where
someone *just like them* managed to find the courage to conquer
it, and where someone was pushed to the limit but didn't curl up
in a little ball and whimper—they dug deep and found inner
resources they didn't know they had. And as the audience walk
away, they might think to themselves, 'You know what? I would
have been terrified too, but maybe next time I'm pushed to the

edge and I feel like I can't cope I can dig deep and find a little bit more too.'

I once heard a sportsperson give what was almost an excellent speech to a group of businesspeople. For the first half an hour she did everything right. She talked about various principles of success, illustrating each one with an example from her own sporting life. The crowd loved it. And then, at the end, she talked about the future of her sport. Now the audience were interested in her sport, but ultimately, like all of us, they cared more about their own lives. If, instead of talking about her sport at the end, she had talked about the audience and drawn a line of connection between the content of her speech and their lives, it would have been a fantastic speech. She should have tied up everything she said in a neat bundle and told them how the principles of success she had outlined could make a difference to her audience too. She could have told them, she should have told them, how they could take the principles that had helped her and apply them to what they were doing in their own lives.

Involving the audience: asking questions

Another way of keeping your listeners interested is to treat them not as if their job is to passively receive information, but as if you and they are on a journey of discovery. You can do this by asking questions. They can be real questions to which you actually let the audience respond, or they can be rhetorical questions, where you ask a question, pause for a moment and then give the answer yourself.

Questions that the audience actually answer can be used effectively sometimes, but the audience has to be small and relaxed enough to participate. In a large audience, most people won't hear an answer given from the floor, which means the speaker has to repeat it. This can get clumsy.

Asking rhetorical questions is a very effective way of getting the audience *to feel* involved. If you say, 'In 1861 the American civil war began', you are imparting information in a straightforward and dull way. But if you say, 'Then in 1861, what happened?' and pause, you will get people's attention—because when we are asked a question our natural impulse is to try to answer it. At least subconsciously, everyone will wonder if you are actually going to pick them out and ask them to answer. They will start preparing what they will say if they are picked. All of a sudden, you have their minds working. They are no longer passive. They are all thinking, 'What's the answer? What did happen in 1861?' When after a moment you say, 'In 1861 the American civil war broke out', they'll all think, 'Of course. I knew that.'

Merely by rephrasing a statement and turning it into a rhetorical question, you can involve your audience to a higher degree. The more questions you ask, the more the audience will feel involved in your talk, and the more involved they feel, the more attentive and receptive they will be.

Imagine being in an audience and being told:

> *The only way to get through the jungle without being killed by a wild animal is to hire a reliable guide.*

Boring. Why not say:

> *What is the only way to get through the jungle without being killed by a wild animal?*

Then leave time for them to think.

'I don't know,' they might wonder. 'What is the only way? Is it to take a particular track? Or do you have to wear a special protective suit?'

Then leave a couple more seconds, and they will think, 'Maybe he's going to ask someone in the audience. What if it's me? What'll I say?'

Then give the answer.

> *The only way is to hire a reliable guide.*

They are involved. You have given them work to do.

Here's another example of keeping your listeners involved by giving them work to do. Say you were giving a speech aimed at training people in retail customer service. You could say this:

> *If you were confronted by a customer who wasn't entitled to a refund but who refused to leave until she got one, the correct procedure would be to call security.*

Again, information is being imparted in a straightforward, boring way.

Why not ask:

> *What would you do if you were confronted by a customer who wasn't entitled to a refund but who refused to leave until she had got one?*

Then leave them enough time to think about it and work out what they would do. Essentially, what you are doing is building tension and making the audience want to know what happens next. If appropriate, you could even take suggestions before you gave them the answer. You'd probably get a range of interesting suggestions, some of which would be good, some of which would be bad, some of which would be funny. A lot of them might throw up interesting, relevant issues for discussion.

If you ask your audience to solve problems, rather than just tell them what to do, they will feel that they are a part of a dynamic, interactive experience.

Creating tension

All good stories involve tension. The tension may be obvious, as when we are wondering whether the hero tiptoeing around the dark house at night is going to be attacked by the murderer, or subtle, as in a good love story, when the tension is created by our wanting to know whether the potential lovers will get together. In fact, usually we know they *will* get together, but the tension is created because we don't know *how* they will get together. If you can create tension, you give your audience a good reason to keep listening. If you can raise a question in their minds, and signal the likelihood that you will answer it, they will keep paying attention to find out the answer.

When tension is created in a movie, we are being manipulated. The scene where the hero is tiptoeing around the dark house doesn't *need* to be drawn out for three minutes; it isn't necessary to advance the story, because nothing is happening. To advance the story we need to know what happens next, that is, whether the murderer will leap out of the shadows and attack the hero. That's what we are waiting for. And the film-maker makes us wait. The scene is drawn out for three minutes because the film-maker knows we are hooked. He has baited the trap by setting up an earlier scene that tells us there is some danger in the house, then having the hero enter it regardless, and now he is reeling us in. Having got us sitting on the edges of our seats, feeling the fear and the tension, why not milk the scene for all it's worth?

One rule the film-maker and the speech-maker must be aware of is this—the pay-off has to be in proportion to the amount of tension built up. If we spend those three minutes watching the hero slink through the house, with scary music and a big build-up, and then the pay-off turns out to be that there is actually no one there and our hero just shrugs his shoulders and goes home, the build-up has been too big for the pay-off. The audience will be dissatisfied.

Let's apply this to public speaking. You should always be on the lookout for ways in which to create tension, to build up that tension and then, eventually, to release it. If you can create tension, the audience will keep listening. If you can give them a mystery ('Is the hero tiptoeing around the house going to be attacked by the murderer?') they will want to know how it is solved.

How do you do that? Well, if you were giving a talk on 'The history of the United States in the twentieth century', you could say, 'There were three pivotal moments in US history in the twentieth century.' Immediately you have created tension. People want to know what those three moments were. In fact, they are already guessing. Was one entering World War I? Or the stock-market crash of 1929? Or Pearl Harbor? Or JFK's assassination, or entering Vietnam, or Watergate, or the release of *Star Wars*?

Having told the audience that there were three pivotal moments in twentieth-century US history, a poor public speaker would immediately say what they were. The result? All tension disappears and the audience returns to being bored.

A good public speaker would leave the identity of the three moments hanging as a tease, and maybe even drop another tease (for example, 'and there were also three people who changed the course of American history'), then would go back and describe what sort of a place the United States was in 1900. While she was doing that she would know that people were going to listen to her every word because they wanted to make sure they didn't miss what those three pivotal events were.

A little bit later the speaker would get to the first of the three pivotal events and talk about it. Later still she'd get to the second one, and finally near the end of her speech she'd talk about the third one. As a result, even if her speech were dull, she would have allowed the tension she created in the first minute to assist in keeping the audience's attention for the whole talk.

Remember that when you use tension in this way, the bigger the build-up and the longer you make the audience wait, the better the pay-off has to be for them. So if you say right at the start that there are three pivotal events in twentieth-century US history, then make the audience wait until the end of your speech to reveal them, you will need to make your argument for choosing those three moments fairly impressive. That is, if you build something up to be one of the centrepieces of your speech, you can't then gloss over it in a few quick words, because you will leave your audience feeling cheated.

There are opportunities to create tension everywhere, even in speeches on seemingly dull subject matter:

- *There is a way to change a car tyre. A simple way that any of you can learn in five minutes. In fact, five minutes from now everyone in this room will have learnt it. But first, I want to tell you what car tyres are made of.*
- *There was once a man who seemingly had everything. He had a beautiful house full of wonderful things, a wife and children, a great job, lots of money and fine friends. And yet he left it all and moved to the other side of the world. Why?*

- *One of the most powerful tools a public speaker can use is the creation of tension. If you know how to create tension you can make even the dullest subject matter seem absolutely fascinating. So how do you do it? Well in five minutes' time you'll know the answer.*

When you talk, raise questions and don't answer them immediately. Create tension by leaving them hanging, either until a later part of your talk or by just pausing for two or three seconds, long enough to give your audience a chance to figure out an answer to the mystery you have set up. Make them lean forward in their eagerness to know. Then, when you tell them, they'll think, 'Yes! I get it!'

Make sure you do answer the questions, though. Remember that unsatisfied feeling when you walk out of a movie and there's one big loose end that hasn't been tied up? Yuk.

Humour

A little bit of humour goes a long, long way. If you can, just every now and again, say something even mildly amusing, it helps enormously in keeping an audience's attention. People love laughing. If you can make them laugh once, they will keep listening in the hope you will do it again. Used properly, humour doesn't work at odds with the aims of your speech, it works in harmony with them. It helps you get your message across. Humour is not something frilly and unimportant around the edges of a speech, it is a tool you can use to make you a better public speaker. If you can give people one good laugh, it will usually be the first thing they remember afterwards. And hearing an audience laugh at something you have said feels great.

Is it hard to be funny? Not as hard as you think. Audiences want to laugh. They love having the opportunity to do so. If their expectation is that they are going to be on the receiving end of a serious speech, and you surprise them by offering an opportunity to laugh, they will leap at it. You can almost hear their relief, the collective thought, 'Thank goodness, we're going to get the odd laugh from this one. Great!'

Trying to be funny is a journey into uncertainty. You can never really tell whether something *you* think is funny will be considered funny by your audience. But testing out funny stuff on friends is a waste of time. The group dynamic is so different from the one-on-one dynamic, that asking a friend if something is funny is next to useless. For a whole year I refrained from using one of the funniest jokes I've ever written, because I'd tried it on a friend who didn't think it was funny. One night I thought, 'Bugger it, I'll give it a go', and it brought the house down.

Generally, humour is a lot funnier when spoken than it is on the page. You can write something you think might be funny, then have all sorts of doubts about it, only to find that when you say it aloud the crowd finds it hilarious. Ultimately you have to trust your instincts. If you think something may well be funny then give it a go. If you're wrong you will have learnt something. Your instincts for humour will develop the more you use them. The more you think about saying funny stuff, open your mind to the possibility of it, and practise it, the more you will pick up what things work and what don't. Often this is largely a subconscious process. Describing and analysing humour is difficult.

Never telegraph humour. Don't tell your listeners that the next thing you are about to say will be funny. Don't say, 'Which reminds me of a funny story . . .', because then if the audience doesn't think it's funny, you'll look and feel like a fool. Not only does saying this set you up for a fall, it also tells the audience how you think they should react, rather than letting them make up their own minds. Also, by telling them where you are going you eliminate tension, which is always a bad thing.

You don't have to turn into a comedian to write the funny parts of your speech. There are many different types of humour, and many different approaches to it. There is no one-size-fits-all approach. Everyone in the world with a sense of humour has their own style. If you keep looking for it, slowly but surely you will find the way to express your sense of humour when you are public speaking.

Even if you think you have absolutely no sense of humour, no funny turn of phrase, you might well be wrong. Check. Ask several people you know well if they think you have a sense of humour. A lot of people who don't think they are funny really are.

If you have any kind of a sense of humour, you are quite capable of being funny on stage. All you need to do is to figure out how your sense of humour works off stage, and extend it to work in the same way on stage. By the way, people who have a sense of humour aren't just those who make other people laugh all the time. You might have a fantastic sense of humour, but choose to keep it to yourself. Having a sense of humour is about seeing things in life that you think are amusing. Not necessarily all the time, just now and again. There aren't many of us who don't do that.

Humour should not seem to be added on to your speech. It should arise naturally from what you are saying. But how? The first step toward adding humour to your speech is to keep a lookout for it. Earlier we discussed how once you had gathered all the factual information you needed for your speech, you should then look through your research material for interesting stories and entertaining pieces of information. If you want to add humour, go through everything a third time and look for things that are funny, or could be made to be funny. Look for things that are weird, or incongruous, or ironic, or silly. When you look specifically for opportunities to add humour, you will usually find them. Go through your speech sentence by sentence and look for opportunities to add something amusing. It doesn't have to be hilarious. Mildly amusing will do. If you look hard enough you'll find them, and the audience will thank you for it. For example, if you are talking about bees you could say: 'Bees are incredibly strong. They can fly while carrying half their body weight. I can't even fly carrying nothing.' Or 'Bees are incredibly strong, they can fly while carrying half their body weight. I'm incredibly impressed by that. I mean, I put my back out the other day just trying to open a jar of pickles.'

Look for humour everywhere. There are no subjects or occasions where humour is inappropriate, as long as it is done well. Proof of this is that many funeral eulogies are full of warm humour about the deceased. The only rules are that humour must be done well, and it must be in good taste. Working out what is, and is not, in good taste is tricky. If you think something might be in bad taste, run it by a couple of people and get their opinion. Also, think seriously about who the humour is aimed at. It is far less likely to offend if the speaker is the butt of the joke, rather than, say, someone in the audience. And people will laugh along with jokes at the expense of the powerful more easily than they will at those that poke fun at the weak and vulnerable.

Here are some places to look for humour.

Making fun of the information you are giving

A lot of humour comes from simply telling the truth. If you have to convey a whole lot of information that sounds dull in your speech, don't be afraid to make fun of it, or yourself. For example:

I feel a bit sorry for you having to absorb all these statistics on fluctuations in copper prices over the last ten years, but then again, I spend half my life analysing them so maybe you should feel sorry for me.

Making fun of your expertise

Don't feel that to gain the respect of an audience you have to take yourself, and whatever expertise you have, incredibly seriously. People will react far better if you are prepared to laugh at yourself, and they will realise that doing so displays real self-confidence.

For example:

Yes, I am a lecturer in international geography, which is weird because we have three young kids and so the furthest I've been from home in the last four years is the park up the road . . . still, that park is a fascinating example of quasi-urban cultivated grassland.

Look for little gags in the stories you tell

Going back to our earlier example of the first person to be tried in an Australian court you could say:

When he saw his mother he said, 'I've got some good news and some bad news . . . The good news is that I've done something no one else has ever done before. The bad news is that I've become Australia's first criminal.'

Make fun of your position

If you are the boss you could say:

Thank you for working so hard all year. That is, apart from that one person who's been spending all their time looking at non-work-related Internet sites and sending emails to their friends . . . and yes, we do know who you are . . . Hey, how come when I said that almost everyone in the room looked guilty?

It is important when using humour to be sensitive and not to offend. This is an issue that is especially relevant at wedding and birthday speeches. There may be a whole heap of hilarious stuff that the groom Bill used to get up to when he got drunk but you need to ask yourself whether any of it is going to embarrass Bill or make him uncomfortable. Or anyone else? Maybe Bill is okay with it, but what about the bride? Or Bill's mum. Or the bride's dad?

The function of a speech at a party is to enhance the enjoyment of everyone there, especially those having the party, and to celebrate them. If you make people feel uncomfortable you've failed. There is no benefit to anyone, and quite possibly a fair bit of damage, in doing that. In assessing whether you are crossing the line from humour to offence, be conservative.

If you're unsure, talk to Charlie. Tell him you're thinking of telling the story about the time he got on the bus wearing just his underpants and ask him if he minds, or whether he thinks anyone else would mind.

Sometimes humour doesn't work, and when it doesn't it feels bad. There's no getting away from that, but you can limit the damage. One of the reasons you should never tell people that you are about to say something funny (for example, 'which reminds me of a funny story', 'listen to this, this is hilarious') is that if you set up that expectation and fail to deliver then it's a long way to fall.

Don't pause when you expect people to laugh, because if they don't it's a very awkward silence. If they do laugh then let the laughter interrupt you. Stop, wait and when it dies down start talking again. If you say something you think is going to be funny and no one laughs but—instead of pausing and waiting for the laugh that never comes—you just keep on talking, then most of the people in the audience won't even realise that you have just tried and failed to make them laugh. And that's a good thing.

If a joke fails, it'll feel bad, but try not to show the pain in your face. If you continue to look calm and confident most people won't know that anything has gone wrong. But if your face shows it they will.

If it's obvious that you have just tried and failed to be funny, often the best thing to do is to acknowledge it. If you say 'I actually thought that was going to be funny . . . but obviously I was wrong', then you'll probably get a laugh anyway. If everyone is aware you have made a failed attempt at humour, by acknowledging it you'll let out all the tension that has been created.

The theme

When we studied texts at school such as *1984*, *Pride and Prejudice*, *Macbeth* and *The Crucible*, it was relatively easy to work out what the plot was and who the characters were. But teachers also kept talking about 'theme'. What was the theme, they wanted to know. The theme was what the story was really about. It was never directly expressed, rather it was the idea or ideas that lay behind the words. In *1984*, one theme is that a totalitarian government can erode an individual's freedom. In *Macbeth*, the main theme is that unchecked ambition can bring guilt and downfall.

The idea of a book or a play having a theme is actually a great example of leading the horse to water but not making it drink. The writer tells the story, but resists the temptation to hit people over the head with their ideas. Rather, they must trust that they have expressed themselves well enough for the reader to pick them up.

Most good stories have a theme; it's like icing on a cake, another layer that adds satisfaction. A good speech should unfold like a good story so the audience wants to know what happens next, and many should also have a theme; that is, some underlying notion connected to the 'story'.

In a way, this is just another way of thinking about how your words can connect to your listeners' real lives and how you can allow them to take away something from your speech that they will find useful. The plot of a speech about how to change a car tyre is the description of how it is done. The theme is that we can learn to be more self-reliant and that becoming self-reliant can increase confidence and self-esteem.

The theme of a speech often emerges only right at the end of the process of writing it. Several years ago I wrote a one-man comedy show about my time as a lawyer. The plot was that I studied law at university, worked for a corporate law firm, then worked for a small firm doing immigration law, then worked for Legal Aid, acting for people charged with criminal offences. I worked on the script off and on for six months, but it wasn't until shortly before I first performed it that I suddenly realised what the theme was. The story was about choice. I realised that I had never exercised much choice in becoming a lawyer; I had just sort of drifted into it. It was only when I realised I didn't like being a corporate lawyer that I took matters into my own hands and started actively searching for things that I would find satisfying. As a criminal lawyer, I saw many people addicted to drugs who only managed to get out of the criminal cycle they were in when they were able to make the very difficult choice to break their addiction.

Once I realised what the theme was, all I needed to do was tweak a couple of parts of the script to emphasise the idea of choice a little more, and to change the ending a bit. I didn't want to smash people about the head with it, but I did want to leave some clues as I moved through the show to allow the audience to see the theme slowly emerge. So it was just a matter of placing a bit more emphasis on the moments in the script where choice was an issue.

I ended the show by saying that it was only when I was doing something I didn't like that I had been sufficiently motivated to start making choices that would enable me to take control of my own life, and once I did that I knew I was on the right track—and the same was true for many of my criminal law clients. Then I said that I thought it was important to be aware that just letting the status quo stand is, in itself, a choice and that 'every day we don't *make* a choice, we've *made* a choice'.

It became a far more satisfying show than a lot of cobbled-together jokes about my time in the law would have been. It was about something. People could just have a laugh and leave, but if they wanted to think about something on the way home, there was something there for them.

A theme is different from the aim of the speech. The aim is straightforward. You work out what it is before you start writing, and whenever you get lost you return to it. A theme is unlikely to be obvious at the start. It may not even be obvious once you have written your speech. You may think your speech has no theme. Maybe you're right. But before you make that decision, look a bit harder. Keep asking yourself, 'What is my speech really all about?'

When looking for themes, look for things that will be relevant and affect everyone in the audience. (Note: I say 'everyone in the audience', not 'everyone'. If you have an audience of astronauts, say, maybe a theme will emerge that would be relevant to them, but which would not be relevant to an audience of, say, dentists.)

Keep your eyes open for a theme or a pattern to emerge. Often it won't until you are very familiar with your whole speech, which means until a few days or hours or minutes before you deliver it. That's okay. Finding the theme doesn't mean you have to re-write the whole thing. It just gives you an added layer to play with.

When looking for themes, start by thinking about some of the things most of us think are important. For example, answers to questions like:

- What is life about?
- How do I make my life better?
- How do I get the balance right between work and other stuff?
- Why can't I get more done?
- How do I make more money?
- How do I get better at the things that I do?
- What the heck is going on?
- How the hell do I live my life?

These sound like big, important, waffly questions but they are questions we all think about and try to work out the answers to. They matter. The fact that the questions are big and waffly doesn't mean your speech has to be big and waffly. It just means that it has to have a point, and a point that people care about.

A speech that tells people how to change a flat tyre is not just about tyres. The reason people want to know how to change a flat tyre is that it will make them more self-reliant and help them feel more capable. So it's a mundane subject connected to a big theme. Themes are everywhere if you look for them, and if you find them they make your speech deeper, better and more memorable.

For a boss giving an end-of-year speech to employees, there can be all sorts of possible themes, such as:

- What we do is important.
- Our work practices are outdated and need to be modernised.
- Technology isn't as important as service.
- Service isn't as important as technology.
- Even if we don't like working here, let's face it, it pays the rent.

If your aim is to give a speech on love, perhaps by the time you have written it a pattern will have emerged. Look for it. That could be the theme. Is it, 'Love is powerful but dangerous', or 'Without love, what's the point?', or 'We all spend our lives looking for love', or something else?

In a speech about 'The migratory habits of the North American mountain goat', the themes that could emerge might be: 'Whatever it takes to survive, living creatures will do it', 'Life is hard, then you die', or 'Nature is extraordinary'.

Motivating and inspiring

A lot of speeches have motivation as one of their aims. There are several ways you can motivate people. A boss might say to her workforce, for example:

> It's really important for the company that everyone puts in. We think there is potential for growth in this company and if we grow then there is an opportunity for everyone to benefit in the form of higher wages. If we don't, if people coast along and the company doesn't expand, then wages won't go up, and it may even be that we have to downsize. So let's all pull together.

This speech appeals to greed and fear. Yes—they are effective motivators of human behaviour, but they won't leave anyone feeling inspired. Motivation is more effective if it taps into positive emotions. What really inspires people is hope, or being part of something bigger than they are, or feeling needed and appreciated.

How about this:

> *This company is not about its buildings or its computers or its vehicles. It is about its people. You. And without you this company is nothing. It stops. Thank you for making this company what it is, and I hope that together we can make it something even bigger and better.*

When you are endeavouring to motivate, ask yourself, 'What emotions am I appealing to?' A good talk should inspire. It really should. It should cause those listening to want to do something. It doesn't have to be something huge and vague like making the world a better place. Yes, you can inspire in a broad way, but you can also aim to inspire in a modest and specific way. For example, a history teacher may inspire his audience to want to find out more about the period he was talking about because it sounded so fascinating. Someone giving a talk on changing a car tyre may give listeners enough knowledge that they are inspired, next time they get a flat, to have a go at fixing it themselves. By giving a great speech, you may inspire someone to take up public speaking. (If you give a truly awful speech you may inspire someone to take it up too.)

If a speaker has the ability to inspire, they have the ability to do something very valuable—and that is to influence people's lives. The difference between an entertaining talk and an inspiring talk is that when people leave the former they think 'Gee, that was entertaining, I enjoyed that'; when they leave the latter they think, 'Gee, I enjoyed that, and you know what? Next time I get a flat tyre I'm going to damn well change it myself.' An inspiring speech motivates listeners to want to somehow live their lives a little bit differently.

Many, many speeches are given with the aim of inspiring those listening. If bosses can inspire employees to care more about what they do it will not only lead to an increase in productivity, but every aspect of the workplace will benefit. Coaches of sporting teams are always looking for sources of inspiration. They get past greats in to give pre-match talks; they take their teams to watch *Rocky* movies together; they think of new and radical ways to repeatedly tell their teams exactly the same things ('Play well! Concentrate! Don't drop the ball!'). Why? Because inspiring people works. Get it right and the people listening will do what they do better.

So how do you do it? How do you inspire? One way is to tell your audience your own story. But then you make it about them. This, of course, sounds like a contradiction, but it isn't.

To inspire, firstly you need the right raw materials to work with. We have all lived through events that have tested us to the limit, and where we found reserves we never knew we had. Every one of us has done at least one thing in our lives that was extraordinary.

I don't necessarily mean going to war. You could have been tested to the limit when you went rock-climbing, or during childbirth, or when you had cancer, or when you were with your father when he died, or when you got sacked, or when your partner dumped you, or by being a parent, or when you got lost bushwalking, or when you hit a big problem at work, or when you realised you wanted to change your career at age 35, or when you started a business, got depressed or had a car accident. We have all been tested and if you're reading this book, you've lived to tell the tale.

Whether you think you passed your tests or failed them, people will be interested in hearing about it. When we are tested we learn. We all fear being tested, but we know that one day we will be. We all hope to meet each test with skill and courage, and we love to hear how others coped when they were tested. Or didn't cope.

Pick a time you were tested. Then tell the story. Start at the beginning and go through to the end. Then say what you learned from the experience. If you are honest in the way you tell your story, and about how you faced being tested, the audience will walk the story in your shoes. And if you are humble, rather than didactic, in the way you explain what you learnt from the experience, and stress that you are just a normal everyday person rather than someone with special gifts, then your listeners will relate to you and take on board what you are saying.

For example, if you are telling the story of the time you were attacked by a shark and fought it off, the way to inspire an audience is not to emphasise what a great fighter you are. If you do that people may admire you, but they probably won't be inspired by you. To inspire someone you need to make them think, 'Yes. I could do that, too!' Emphasising what a great fighter you are will make them think, 'I'm not a great fighter, so I guess I could never do that.'

Emphasise, rather, the things we all share, the things that make you human:

> *As the shark came toward me I was terrified. I thought I was going to die. Then as it attacked me, I knew that my only hope was to fight back. I was petrified but out of pure desperation I struck out and somewhere within me I found the strength to fight that shark off. I've never done anything like that before in my life. And I think that maybe*

we all have within us reserves of strength we don't use that we don't even know are there until we need them. And ever since that day I've known I have that extra level within me, and I've tried to tap into it in challenging times. Because I've noticed you meet a few sharks that walk on two legs.

In the first sentence the situation is set up and a bridge of empathy is built by saying what everyone would be thinking: 'I thought I was going to die'. It is such a powerful scenario that the audience will be right there in the water with the speaker. The speaker continues to emphasise that he is just a normal person with the phrases 'I was petrified', 'out of pure desperation' and 'I've never done anything like that before in my life'. Then the lesson is subtly explained. The speaker doesn't go over the top and say, 'We are all full of power! Tap into your hidden powers and rule the world!' Rather, he gently explains what he thinks his experience means and what application it could have for those listening. Finally, humour is used to make the point that the lesson of this experience could have a wider application.

You can inspire without talking about yourself. You can tell stories about others. You can talk about the courage of soldiers, about the perseverance of mountain climbers, about the ingenuity and determination of inventors. Work out what message you want those to whom you are talking to leave with, then work out a way of telling a story with that message.

If you want your audience to leave thinking, 'I am going to re-assess my life and work out what I can do to make it better', tell a story about a person who did just that. Tell them how a person, you or someone else, was drifting along in life, then was one day prompted (by an accident, the death of a loved one, winning the lottery, whatever) to examine her life afresh and to make some changes. That person went on to . . . what? Change the world, invent the wheel, live happily ever after? . . .

If you want your audience to leave thinking that it's amazing what we can all achieve when we work together, tell them a story about a group of people who all worked together and achieved something fantastic.

You don't have to make up the story—find it. There are millions of great stories out there.

You can also inspire without talking about particular people. Simply work out what message you want to send, and work out a way of making it sound attractive. If you want to send the message that a person's destiny is in their own hands, say why you think this is so. Be passionate, logical and persuasive. If you really believe it, you'll probably get there. If you don't really believe it then you probably shouldn't be saying it.

Emotion

We value logic highly in our world, especially in argument. What is often just as persuasive, sometimes more persuasive, is emotion. Emotion is also an enormously effective tool in creating empathy. In the previous story about being attacked by a shark, the key words that make you really tap into and understand what the speaker was going through are, 'I was terrified. I thought I was going to die'. Those simple words put the listener in the speaker's shoes far more effectively than the most eloquent description of what the shark looked like and what it was doing.

Too often we concentrate on talking about what we *think* and don't spend enough time talking about what we *feel*. If you are trying to persuade an audience of something, then of course you need to provide evidence that your point of view has merit, and to build your arguments logically. But don't ignore emotion.

Don't be afraid to tell people how you felt: 'After I escaped the shark and got back to the beach, I crawled up onto the sand, and I felt utterly drained, in shock, but elated too, because I had survived.'

Invite the audience to assess their feelings about what you have said. Earlier, I discussed talking about the first man in space. Ask the audience how that story made them feel. Were they excited and inspired by the achievement? Were they disappointed at the waste of resources? Or something else?

Be as logical as you can be in your efforts to persuade, but use emotion to complement those efforts. Human action is motivated by our feelings rather than our thoughts. Additionally, when you tell people how something made you feel, you implicitly invite them to work out how it makes them feel.

Talking like you talk

What about the words that you use in your speech? How formal should they be? What speaking style should you adopt? When writing a speech should you make any adjustments for the fact that what you are working on is not going to be read by anyone, but listened to?

This may sound weird, but I believe that the most natural way to write a speech is by talking to yourself, then writing down what you have said. That way, what comes out is natural speech. I write the best bits of my speeches while I'm out walking. I imagine myself up there, and imagine myself talking. Then I hurry home and write down what I imagined myself saying.

I certainly work a lot at my computer, but the most natural bits of ready-to-go speech come to me when I'm not writing but talking inside my head. It's sort of like hearing voices—except that the voice, luckily, is my own.

If you work too intimately with the written word when you create a speech, the danger is that when you deliver it you will sound as though you are merely reading out loud. This is one of the most common faults in public speaking. The best speeches do not sound as if the speaker is 'giving a speech'. They sound as if the speaker is just talking. They sound natural. People will relate to you and accept what you say far more easily if you speak with honesty and without artifice, rather than as though you were 'giving a speech'. Aim to speak in exactly the same way as you speak when you are normally talking to people.

Don't talk like you write, don't talk like you think someone giving a speech should talk, don't talk like a stiff, nervous, formal version of yourself. Talk like you talk.

The way most of us write is quite different from the way we talk. The easiest way to understand the difference between how you talk and how you write is to do this exercise. Write a paragraph about anything, say, explaining how to change a car tyre. Wait a while until you have forgotten what you wrote, then tell yourself—in your head—how to change a tyre. Then write down what you just told yourself, and compare the two. Probably they are quite different, not in what they say, but in how they say it.

You might write about changing a tyre like this:

First remove the jack from the boot of the car and place it under the wheel that has the puncture. Before you use the jack to lift the car, loosen the nuts on the wheel two or three revolutions. Ensure the jack is correctly placed on a part of the car that is secure and strong so it won't slip, then pump up the jack—and the car—until the wheel with the puncture is several centimetres clear of the road. Then continue to loosen and remove the nuts and slide the wheel off the car. Replace with the new wheel, then re-attach the nuts. Gently let the car back down to the ground, and then completely tighten the nuts. The job is complete.

And this is how you might say it:

Get the jack out of the boot and put it under the car, and make sure it's sitting somewhere secure. But before you pump the car up, loosen the nuts a couple of turns. Pump the car up until the wheel's off the ground, then finish taking the nuts off. Take the wheel off, put the new one on, replace the nuts, let the car down, tighten the nuts and you're done.

Two different ways of communicating the same information, one appropriate to the written word, one to the spoken word. If you are giving a speech you will communicate far more effectively if you can get people to forget that they are listening to A Speech. What you need to do is to talk to them, just the way you might talk to them in the corridor or at lunch.

As you work out what you are going to say, watch out for those bits of artifice that don't sound natural, that don't sound like how you talk. Get rid of them. Translate them back from written English into spoken English.

Talking like you talk does not limit in any way what you say. It just influences how you say it.

An easy way to make sure that your speech sounds like you talk is to go ahead and write it, then go through it and speak it aloud. You'll pick up all the bits that don't sound like the way you normally talk, and then you can adjust them.

One way of learning to write how you speak is to record yourself talking about something, and then to transcribe it. I'm wary of this method because whenever most of us hear our own voice we think it sounds terrible, and the last thing you need when you are trying to get better at public speaking is to become self-conscious about the sound of your voice. But if you're brave, feel free to do it.

By the way, more on this later, but any type of voice is fine for public speaking, it's how you use it that's important.

Slides

The use of slides and visual aids such as PowerPoint presentations has become enormously common in public speaking. More and more reliance is placed upon them, sometimes to the extent that the slides are written first and then the speech has to fit around them. I'm not a fan of slides. I think sometimes people use them because they lack confidence in their ability to hold an audience's attention and they think some sort of visual distraction will help. Other times, the popularity of slides causes people to assume that they should have them, even if they are not quite sure why.

Understand this. When you are public speaking there is nowhere to hide. You can have as big a screen and as many slides as you like, but like it or not, you will still be judged on how well you speak. I suggest that you save the time you spend on designing slides and spend it instead working out how to give a better speech.

There is no point, in my opinion, in ever putting up words on a slide. Words are what you want the audience to listen to coming out of your mouth. If you want them to read what you have to say, then just hand out copies of your speech and go home.

The only slides that are useful are those that communicate information in a way that is superior to the way you could communicate it with words. For example, if you are talking about a new species of bird just discovered in India, you may want to show a map of India to indicate where exactly the bird has been found, and a picture of the bird. Both would pass the test, being a better way of communicating the information than trying to describe in words where the bird has been found and what exactly it looks like.

One of the most important things to do when public speaking is to minimise distractions. That's why we get the house lights turned down and ask people to turn off their mobile phones. If you put up topic headings or key messages or other words on slides on a big screen, what you are doing is splitting the audience's attention. You are creating distractions. Do you want your audience to read what is up on the screen, or do you want them to pay attention to you? Or do you want them to half do both? (Which is what usually happens.) What sort of message are you sending? The message you should be sending your audience is that every word you say is worth listening to, but if you put on a slide with words, aren't you sending the message that if they listen to you they'll get part of the story, but to really get everything they need to pay attention to the screen? And the more attention they pay to the screen the less attention they pay to you.

I know we live in an era of multi-skilling, where people think they can do five things at a time, but public speaking is about focusing the whole audience's attention on what you are saying. If people are reading from a screen at the same time, they can't pay as much attention to what you say.

It's important for your own confidence, too, that you see your audience is paying attention to you. If they are all looking off to your right at a screen and clearly paying more attention to it, your confidence can go out the window.

I don't deny that graphs and other diagrammatic rendering of information can be very useful, but don't over-complicate things. I suggest that you put up the slide, explain why it's there, then get rid of it. If you're not talking about it, it shouldn't be there. And you should lead the audience through it. For example, put up the slide, then:

> *That's an Indian elephant. Have a look at that long nose, that's called a trunk, and they use that for grabbing food. See the tusks. They're sharp. What an animal.*

Slide off.

> *Next, the mongoose.*

If you are going to use slides, use them only when they are a better communication tool than words. Don't have words on them. And get them up there, explain what's going on, then get them off.

Having said that, sometimes slides can be just the thing. For example, using slides in birthday or wedding speeches can be very effective. Especially when the slides are used as the punch lines of jokes. For example, 'Anne was always a neat, clean child'—reveal slide of Anne aged six covered in mud.

If you are the MC of an awards night there may be lots of audio-visual support, such as slides and background music. Typically, there will be 20 or 30 awards to present and a slide will come up as you read out the nominees and there will be background music to cover the time it takes for the winner to walk up on stage to collect their award. Make sure you talk to the person who is controlling it all before the show. Ask them to make sure that the information on the slides comes up on the screen a beat *after* you say it, not beforehand or at the same time. If the information comes up before you say it, or at the same time, people have no need to pay attention to you. They'll just look at the screen. So make sure it follows you.

If there is background music, make sure it's faded down to zero before anyone starts speaking. You should never have to speak over music. It is a major distraction for the audience. And you shouldn't have to wait for the music to fade down. Ask the controllers to keep an eye on you, so that when you lean in to start speaking they cut the music immediately.

Jargon

The world has become jargon-heavy, awash in words and phrases that are only used and understood by members of a particular group. It's usually job-related. Engineers, managers, builders and biologists all have their own specific jargon, language they use that relates specifically to their work. Some jargon is useful, specialised language, but much of it just involves using words not many people understand when it would be much simpler to use words that everyone understands. What jargon can easily do is exclude. If you use a jargon word or phrase and someone in the audience doesn't understand it, they will feel excluded. In addition, it will operate as a distraction, as the left-out audience member will be trying to work out what the jargon means. So don't use jargon unless you know everyone in the room understands it, and even then don't use it unless it is clearly the *best* way to communicate.

However, it is good to speak the language of the people you are talking to. Company directors at a conference use different language to 20-year-olds in a pub. Many people subconsciously alter their speech to match that of the person they are speaking to. They will choose different words, and even subtly alter their speaking voice, depending on whether they are speaking to a priest or a builder's labourer. There's nothing wrong with this. The aim is sensible—to maximise the chance that what you say will be understood. So when you speak to a group work out who they are, listen to how they communicate, and adjust how you speak accordingly.

Verbal tics

Try to keep track of the stock words and phrases that you use. Most of us develop some form of verbal tic; a word or phrase that we continually return to, often unconsciously. For example, 'you know'. Other tics people often develop are 'and so on', and 'and so forth'. They are usually words or phrases that don't mean much at all and don't add anything to what we are saying. We use them to buy ourselves some time to try and work out what we are going to say next.

Do you have any verbal tics? Are there any words or phrases that you repeat over and over again without realising it? Try to spot what they are, because if you don't, the audience will, and it will distract them and make you appear less in control and less competent. Ask someone who listens to you a lot to tell you what your verbal tics are. It might be painful, but it's worth it. I have kept myself amused through many a dull speech by identifying the stock, often meaningless phrases the speaker keeps repeating and keeping a tally of how often they are repeated. You don't want someone to be doing that to you.

The end

How do you end a speech? Do you keep going until you've run out of things to say and then stop? Do you summarise what you have said?

Just like goodbyes, endings can be awkward. The principle is simple. You want to end on a high. You want to hit a big up in your speech, where you have the audience's complete attention and they think what you are saying is wonderful and that, in fact, *you* are wonderful, and then shut up and get off before you stuff it up and give them the opportunity to change their minds.

Those moments are hard enough to create at any time, but to conjure one up right at the end of your speech is doubly difficult. But it can be done.

I am not a big fan of the end-of-speech summary. Good stories don't need to tell you what happened earlier. Good books or films don't end with a re-cap of the entire plot. If your speech has worked, people won't need a summary. They'll remember. If it hasn't worked, a summary won't fix it.

I believe one of the best ways to end a speech is to do this:

1. Pick up the theme, or one of the themes, that you have raised in your speech.
2. Tell a story that illustrates the theme.
3. Make it clear to the audience how what you have said in points 1 and 2 is relevant to them.
4. Tell them why what you have said in your speech is important; and
5. Set them a challenge.

For example, let's return to the speech on 'How to change a car tyre'. Not at first glance an easy subject to extract a theme from and craft an inspirational ending. But, as we discussed earlier, it's not what your speech is about, it's how you approach it that's important.

This could be an ending:

> *After you have tightened the nuts on the wheel, you remove the jack, put it back in the car and you're ready to go. You've changed the tyre.*
> *(PAUSE.)*

I was once driving on a deserted dirt road in pouring rain, out of mobile phone range, when I got a flat tyre. Back then, I had no idea how to change a car tyre. I remember the incredible feeling of frustration I felt as the rain poured down on my head and I looked at all these tools in the boot, and didn't have any idea how to use them. I sat in that car for four hours waiting for another car to come, but that wasn't the worst bit. The worst bit was when eventually another car did come, and seeing the contemptuous expression on the face of the driver when I told him I needed help to change a tyre. I'll never forget that expression and I hope you never experience it, or if you have you never experience it again.

You can't learn how to change a car tyre by listening to me tell you how to do it. Listening to me may have given you the knowledge, but if you want to be confident you can do it, you'll need to practise. Good luck.

The themes here are independence and self-reliance. The story illustrates the importance of each. The story is relevant to the audience because it warns of the dangers of not being able to change a car tyre, and in the audience are people who have come to find out how to change a car tyre. The challenge to them is to take away the knowledge they have gained and apply it. The challenge is very important, as it makes it clear to those in the audience that the journey they began by coming and listening to the speech is not over. There is more work to be done. By setting the challenge of going away and applying what they have learnt, there is a symbolic handing-over of power from the speaker to the listeners. Ideally, at the end of the speech, the listeners are inspired to act. In this case, they walk out of the room determined to go home and practise changing a car tyre.

The great thing about ending with a personal anecdote that illustrates your theme is that it reinforces what you have been saying in your speech *without* repeating it. At the end of your speech you want to make sure your audience has got your main points. That's why so many people do summarise at the end; they want to make sure the audience gets it. But telling a new, fresh story is a far more interesting and exciting way to convey information. At the end of a speech would you rather hear this:

> *To repeat, it is important to know how to change a car tyre to be self-reliant, and the main things to remember in changing a car tyre are these . . .*

Or this?

> *I was once driving on a deserted dirt road in pouring rain, out of phone range, when I got a flat tyre . . .*

The first is a lecture—even worse, in fact, it's a repeat of a lecture. The second is a story that makes the listener want to know what happens next. And the beauty of it is that every sentence of the story is operating in the same way that a summary does. That is, the story reinforces the key information in the speech.

Another good way to end a speech is to simply focus on why what you have been talking about is important. Let's go back to the example of a talk instructing salespeople on how to sell the new mobile phone that contains a video camera and hair dryer. Here's a possible ending:

> *Some of you might think this product is a bit of a gimmick and to be honest for a while I thought that too. But then I found out that one of our customers who bought one had*

gone out bushwalking and had been bitten by a snake. She managed to film the snake with her phone as it slithered away. As soon as medics got to her, she showed them the film, they knew exactly what sort of snake it was, and could give her the right serum. If there had been a delay while they tried to work it out, she may have died. I'm not saying that this new phone is going to save the life of everyone who buys it, but you may want to bear that story in mind when you're thinking about how useful it is.

The message is this: what the speaker has been talking about is important. If you can leave the audience thinking that, you have done well.

Here's another potential ending to a speech given by a boss at an end-of-year function:

I was talking to a friend the other day and he was complaining about how much he disliked his job. As he was talking I suddenly realised that where we work is somewhere I do enjoy being, and where I do feel that I can be myself and where I feel challenged by my work. And it struck me that I was pretty lucky. I hope you feel that way about where we all work, too. I hope that you think it's a good place to be. If you don't, come and talk to me about it and we'll try and fix it. And there's one more thing I hope. I hope that we can all make this an even better place.

Now while this is a story about the speaker, there is a very strong message for the audience. But note that the speaker doesn't tell anyone what to think. She isn't telling the audience they should feel lucky, she is just saying that she feels lucky and is inviting them to similarly examine their circumstances. Then she challenges them to make the place where they work even better.

A headmaster ending a speech at a school speech day might tell a story about a particular student who had arrived at the school shy but who had gradually come out of his shell and blossomed to take the lead in the school play. A guest from outside the school might end her speech by talking about the things she wished someone had told her when she was finishing school.

A final word on endings: sometimes you can hit a perfect moment to end before you planned to end. You will suddenly feel that you have made your point and the audience have got it. If you are lucky enough to hit a great moment like that then, unless there's a really good reason not to, get off. Many is the time I have stumbled across a perfect moment to end a speech on, but not realised it at the time and kept going, only to end a few minutes later on a sliding anti-climax.

Finally, ask yourself these questions:

- Does my speech tell a story? Is there a beginning, a middle and an end?

- Have I used tension and suspense to keep the audience interested?

- Will my speech matter to the audience? Does it contain material that will be relevant to their lives?

- Does it inspire? Does it motivate?

- Are there enough examples to bring what I am saying to life?

- Does it contain any humour?

- Is there a theme?

- When I read it aloud does it sound like a 'Speech'? Or does it sound like me talking?

- Does it contain jargon that people may not understand?

- Does my speech have a big finish?

- Have I fulfilled the aim I started with when I answered the question 'why am I speaking?' (If not, you either need to change your speech or change your topic.)

three

BEFORE YOU SPEAK

You're there (and ready?). You've done the work (haven't you?), you know your topic (don't you?) and now the time has come. Nearly. You are to give your speech in one hour's time. So what should you do until then? Go over your notes? Rewrite the bits that sound clumsy? (But what if the whole thing sounds clumsy?) Should you pace up and down? Or sit calmly and meditate? Or pace up and down while meditating? Or drink? Not much, just one to calm your nerves. Or two.

You get up and pace, then sit, then look at your notes, then pace some more, then go to the toilet, then sit and try to go over your notes, but after a while realise you're just staring blankly at the paper while, all the time, your mind is just saying—no, not saying, screaming—one thing: AAARRRRRRRGHHH!!!

The set-up

Make sure you arrive at the place you are speaking early enough to check out the set-up before the function begins—*especially* if it's the first time you've been there! Sometimes you can pick up things that are wrong and adjust them (or get them adjusted), and it makes your job a lot easier. In fact, not sometimes—often.

The speaker's performance usually needs to begin the moment he or she walks in the door. The person who has asked you to speak, and the organisers, and everyone else who has a stake in your talk going well, will be nervous. They will want it to go well. They will want you to go well. They will be scared that you won't go well. They will be wondering whether perhaps they should have asked someone else. They will scrutinise you. They will check you out.

The best way to reassure them is to act relaxed and confident from the moment you walk through the door. Be polite, smiley and approachable. Try to appear cool, calm and collected—which you probably won't be. In fact, you almost definitely won't be, because you will be walking into an unfamiliar environment, often meeting people you don't know, and on the verge of exposing yourself publicly to the judgment and scrutiny of others. I get nervous enough walking into a party alone.

If you are obviously nervous, the organisers will pick up on it, and that will make *them* even more nervous. They'll keep asking you how you are, and fussing, and that will make *you* even more nervous, which will make *them* more nervous—a vicious circle. So it's important to try to project an air of unflappable calm from the word go. If you can be relaxed and friendly and do a bit of bonding with the people running the show early on, then later, when you ask them to do something, such as move the position of the stage, they will be more likely to do it.

The other benefit of pretending that you are utterly relaxed and confident is that the more relaxed and confident you act the more relaxed and confident you will actually become.

But how do you act relaxed and confident when you aren't? I'll be saying more about nerves later on, so you can put into practise the techniques I outline there. Basically—slow down, walk slowly, be friendly and polite, and don't rush what you say or what you do. If you act calm, you will be calm. Or at least calmer than you would otherwise be.

Be on the lookout for things that are set up badly and which will make your job harder. For example, the stage could be in the wrong place, the microphone at the back corner of the stage rather than in the middle, the sound system not working properly. Most problems are fixable, but you need to be delicate.

Ask to have a look at the place where you'll be giving your talk. And have a good hard look.

The stage

Firstly, go up onto the stage. Check it out. Get the feel of it. Are there any steps to trip on or things to bump into? I once began my role as MC at a very posh black tie dinner by tripping on a step and going flying across the stage. I only just caught my balance before I face-planted, and tried to act as if nothing had happened. Afterwards someone said they thought it was both deliberate and hilarious. It was the nearest I've ever come to physical comedy in my life.

Make sure that the point you are speaking from is as close to the front and centre of the stage as possible. It's hard to dominate an audience if you are not even dominating the stage.

Nowadays, because of the obsession many speakers have with slides, the speaking position is often right on the very edge of the stage, and dwarfed by a huge projection screen. Even if you are using slides, the main focus of attention should always be you. It's not a PowerPoint presentation that is aiming to engage and stimulate an audience, it's you. So if the lectern has been put in a corner of the stage to make way for the screen, try to get it moved. Even if other speakers need it there, ask them to move it for your speech. If you are showing slides, and a front and centre speaking position would mean that you are in the way of the audience having a clear view of the slides, just step briefly to the side of the stage whenever you put one up.

There are other reasons why your speaking position may not be front and centre. At some functions it's because musicians will be playing from the same stage. However, if you explain that having the lectern tucked away in the corner will make life more difficult for all those speaking, usually a compromise can be worked out. Often it's as simple as removing the lectern after the speakers finish and before the band starts.

Check out the sightlines, too. Make sure you can see every part of the audience. If you can't see them they can't see you. It is very hard to engage the attention of people who can't see you. Go and sit at the back to check how well you can see the stage. If some people's view is obscured by a pillar, you can't move the pillar, but you may be able to move the chairs.

If you can't do that then, depending on how long you are speaking for, you may want to ask the person introducing you to ask those behind the pillars to move their chairs so they can see you.

In general, you want to be as close to the audience as possible. That's why it's good to be at the front of the stage. It's also good to be central to the audience, so if 80 per cent of your audience will be to your left, move your speaking position to the left of the stage.

Ideally, the nearest members of the audience should be just a couple of metres away from your speaking position. Unfortunately, particularly at night-time functions, there's often a dance floor between you and the audience. When you are separated from the audience by an ocean of empty dance floor, it's going to be a lot harder to get their attention. The further away from the audience you are the harder it gets. Often you just have to live with the dance floor situation.

One thing that I've done several times with success is to set up my mike stand off the stage, at the front of the dance floor to be nearer to the audience. As long as you don't need the height of the stage to see the people at the back I'd recommend it. Sometimes, as long as you are very nice to the organisers, you can get the stage moved, especially if it's just a riser.

If you do a bit of public speaking you'll soon get a feel for all this, and you'll be able to smell a good room and a bad room right away.

And difficult circumstances can bring out the best in you. I once did a 40-minute comedy spot at 10.45 p.m. at a function in Perth. Already that's way too late to go on, but in addition I had woken up in Hobart that morning and the three-hour time difference effectively made it 1.45 a.m. for me. I had woken at 6.00 a.m. east coast time, and for the two hours before I went on I had been walking round in circles in my hotel room upstairs, slapping myself in the face and drinking coffee to avoid falling asleep. When I finally saw the room (I had broken my own rule and not had an earlier look) I thought Moses must have been on before me. In front of the stage was a 10-metre wide channel of emptiness that ran right to the back of the room. For some reason the audience had been parted. In front of me there was no one, but to my far left were a hundred people, and to my far right were another hundred. To see one half I had to turn my back three-quarters to the other half.

So when I went on I played audience tennis. If anyone had taken a video of me it would have looked as though I was watching the longest rally in the history of the sport. I alternated; set up to the left hand side, punch line to the right, then set up to the right and punch line to the left. I came off with a cricked neck and utterly knackered—but at least it all worked. Thank goodness—4000 kilometres is a long way to go to fail.

Lights and sound

Ask about the lights. If there are any sound and lighting people, introduce yourself, remember their names and make friends with them. The best lighting for public speaking is to have very bright light on you, and very little or no light anywhere else. If the lighting reinforces the point that there is one point of focus, which is the person on the stage, it will help. Try to get the house lights dimmed when you go on.

Watch out for other distracting lights. At a nightclub where I was about to do stand-up I had to ask: 'When I go on, do you mind turning the mirror ball off?' A continuum of multicoloured spotty lights drifting across my face might have been a tad distracting. It's all about focus, about making it as easy as possible for the audience to pay attention to you.

Check the sound too. Usually it will be fine, but it's good to get someone to say a few words into the microphone while you sit at the back. Some mikes distort if you have them too close your mouth, others you almost have to swallow for them to pick you up.

Audience set-up

The more tightly packed an audience is, the more responsive, relaxed and at ease its members will feel. If they are packed tight, they will feel warm and safe, like rabbits in a warren. Their proximity to each other creates a vibe. Spread out, they will feel lonely, separated and vulnerable. Thus you get a better reception with theatre-style seating than when your audience is seated around tables.

A packed room has a much better vibe than a room that is half empty. And 50 people can either pack a room full or leave it half empty. It all depends on how many seats there are. Fifty people spread over 100 seats looks empty and sad. People will wonder why they are there, and what the 50 people who didn't come knew that they didn't. But 50 people sitting in 50 seats feels like a full house, and a full house creates an expectation and gets people thinking (perhaps only subconsciously, but that's enough), 'Gee, weren't we lucky to get a seat?'

> However many people are in the audience, you need to make it look like a packed house. It's quite easy. Count the number of seats. Ask how many people will be in the audience. Then get rid of the excess seats.

If you are speaking, say, in a lecture theatre that holds 200, and 125 are expected, simply block off the back third of seats. If you are in a room with 80 individual seats, and you are expecting 50 people, remove the excess seats.

Another advantage of removing or cordoning off seats is that when you have a lot more seats than people, you will usually find that as many people as possible sit toward the back. (The only time people voluntarily try to get a seat up the front is when they're going to see a band.) Rooms fill from the middle, then the back, then the last people in get the seats at the front. If there are too many seats, you'll be looking at two or three rows of nothing, which means you'll be further away from the audience, which will make your job more difficult.

Getting what you want

Mistakes in setting up aren't usually the result of anything other than a slight lack of knowledge and experience. When the advantages of getting things right are explained to someone in a calm and logical matter, problems can usually be fixed. Some speakers make the mistake of complaining about how badly a venue is set up without ever asking for the problems to be solved. That doesn't help.

When you want a last-minute change to anything, be delicate. The organisers are probably feeling anxious about how things will go and the last thing they want is extra hassles. First, tell them how great it all looks and how much you're looking forward to the gig. Then point out the problem you have noticed and say you were just wondering if it was possible that we—note 'we' not 'you'; reinforce the fact that you are all in this together—could make this small change because (and this is important) you believe that it would significantly improve the evening for everyone attending. Then tell them why it will improve the evening. If you can convince them that they need to make a change or the evening *as a whole* will suffer, there is a much greater likelihood that you'll get the stage moved or the house lights turned down or whatever else it is you want. Ensure you don't give the impression that you are being precious (and if you are anxious, it's very easy to give that impression) and emphasise that your main concern is that the audience enjoys the evening as much as possible. For example: 'It would be a shame if those people whose view is currently blocked by that pillar weren't able to enjoy what's going on'.

Nervousness, and how to control it

I find the most frequently asked question about public speaking is, 'Do you get nervous?' My answer is 'Yes, but less than I used to'. Public speaking is one of humanity's greatest fears, and it's quite natural to get nervous before you do it. But there are ways of controlling your nerves and there are two very good reasons to learn how to do so.

The first is that to be a good public speaker you need to be able to project a sense of calm authority. You need to appear to be in complete control and at ease. If you can do that, your audience will relax and come along for the ride. They will accept that you are where you are meant to be and doing what you are meant to be doing and they will pay attention. But if you are obviously nervous, if you are fidgeting and look uncomfortable, this will quickly affect the entire audience. The more uncomfortable the speaker feels, the more uncomfortable the audience will feel, and the more easily they will lose respect and stop paying attention. When a speaker looks and acts nervous, things can rapidly go downhill.

The second reason it is important to learn how to control your nerves is that it's really unpleasant to spend a lot of time being nervous. At its worst it's a feeling of dread that something you desperately don't want to happen (to go on and give your speech) is, nonetheless, going to happen. Time drags, and because you are consumed by anxious thoughts, you can't prepare properly. You can't eat, you pace and fidget, and by the time you get on stage you're drained. Yuk. If you need or want to be doing a lot of public speaking it's important that you don't spend a lot of your life feeling like that.

I am talking about controlling your nerves, not eliminating them. I don't know whether it's possible to entirely eliminate all feelings of nervousness, but even if it were, I'm not sure it would be a good idea. Nervousness stimulates us, and if we can learn how to use it, it can help us get fired up and focused. What we want is to reduce the negative effects of nervousness, and also to ensure that when we are on stage we don't appear to the audience to be nervous.

Why does public speaking worry people so? Why is it so often one of our greatest fears? There is no physical danger, and even if the speech is a disaster it's not really going to stuff up your life. So what's the big deal?

Public speaking is public performance, and public perform-ance with nowhere to hide. You can't blame the writer or the director or anyone else, because what you are doing is entirely your own work. When you give a speech, you are asking people to judge you. And the jury is right there in front of you. If your audience doesn't like what you say, or the way in which you say it, they will feel contempt for you for wasting their time, and you will see that contempt on their faces.

We all want to be accepted, we all want to be loved, and one of the rewards of good public speaking is that you do feel accepted and loved by a whole group of people you have never even met. If feels great. But the flip side is that every time we speak we risk public humiliation and rejection. And when that happens, it hurts. It is that fear of public humiliation and rejection that creates the stakes of public speaking, and what makes us nervous. Fear of failure.

The effects of nervousness

Whatever the cause, most people feel nervous before they perform. Don't worry, it's normal. Being a little nervous can be helpful as it gets the adrenalin flowing—and that will have you aroused and peaking for your speech. But our nervous response was developed to help us to run away from sabre-toothed tigers, and so a surge of adrenalin bursting through your body gives you lots of energy. It makes you feel like moving, which is good if a tiger is chasing you, but not so good if you have to sit around waiting for your turn to talk. To get rid of that nervous energy, we fidget, pace, jiggle our legs, talk too much, become dry-mouthed, drink glass after glass of water, and unconsciously rip all our notes into hundreds of tiny pieces. (I did that standing outside my final year school English exam. I looked down and realised that all the *Macbeth* quotes I had brought to learn at the last minute were lying in shreds on the ground.)

When we are nervous we also find it difficult to concentrate. Instead of using the time before we go on stage to get ready we can work ourselves into such a state that sometimes we've lost the battle before it's begun.

On stage the most obvious effects of being nervous are shaking hands, a quavering or trembling voice that is pitched higher than usual, and fidgeting. We may speak too fast and lose our natural sense of timing. We might breathe too shallowly and too quickly so that the only sound we can make is a high-pitched squeak with no authority.

Not only does each of these potential effects make it harder to deliver a speech, they also telegraph your state of mind to the audience. When the audience sees that you are nervous, it makes them nervous too. When a speaker is obviously edgy, the audience will doubt their competence. It's like being on a plane and hearing the pilot say, 'Well, I guess we'll try to take off now. Wish me luck.'

If you are feeling nervous on stage, instead of focusing on being in the moment and delivering your speech, you may experience a curious, unsettling sensation of being removed from yourself, as if you're hovering outside your body watching yourself like a spectator, unable to quite connect with yourself or the audience.

Worst of all, you may go blank. You may completely forget everything you have to say and have to crawl from the stage humiliated. I did that in one of my first stand-up comedy appearances. It feels bad, very bad. Even if you have notes you may end up just reading them out stutteringly and blankly.

If you get nervous, then welcome to the human race. It's natural. It's also quite possible to control your nervousness, and to learn how to use it to your benefit. You need to control the outward signs of nervousness. And if you can control the outward signs, you'll be surprised how quickly the internal effects recede, too.

Controlling nervousness

The trick is to use your nervous energy positively. Everyone knows that a good performer is relaxed, in control, confident and natural, but how do you learn to exhibit those qualities?

The first thing you can do is to be thoroughly prepared. One of the biggest fears nervousness attaches to is that of being in front of an audience and forgetting what you are going to say. You imagine yourself standing out there with your mind completely blank. If you are going to be using notes, you should be able to reassure yourself that if your mind does go blank, as long as you retain the ability to read you will be okay. But what if your speech is meant to be fully or partly memorised? The better you know your speech, the harder it is to forget it. If you know your speech back to front and upside down, the idea of suddenly forgetting it completely becomes as ridiculous as the idea of not being able to remember what day of the week it is.

When you have written out your speech, and you're nervous, it's tempting to treat those pages with their printed words as your speech. That sheaf of papers is not your speech. It is merely what you have written your speech down on. Your speech is the accumulation of all the knowledge you have about the subject you are speaking on, and all the work you have done in shaping it into the words you are going to say. Your speech is in your head.

I rely on notes a lot, but once I left a fully typed-up speech at home. I realised what I'd done 20 minutes before I went on—and I was meant to speak for 20 to 30 minutes! I quickly wrote down as many of the main points as I could remember, but even so, instead of going on with seven pages typed on paper, I went on with 25 words scribbled on a napkin. The speech went fine. I had done the work. I knew what I wanted to say. It was all in my head.

When you know your subject matter well, the idea of going blank becomes unthinkable. Suppose I asked you to stand up right now and with no preparation talk for 20 minutes about your life so far—you could do it. If I asked you whether you had any fear of going blank you'd probably laugh at me. You know the subject. You are an expert on it. If you do enough work beforehand so that you feel you are an expert on the subject of your talk, the confidence that creates will mean that you will not get as nervous.

When you're battling nerves, try to remember that the worst thing that can happen isn't really all that bad. Even if the speech does go badly, you will still be alive and healthy, and you may even still get paid. Treat the opportunity to deliver a speech as something important, but if it doesn't go well, who really cares. (However, I must admit, unfortunately, that this strategy doesn't always work. Rationally it makes sense, but it is very hard to get rid of the terror that the fear of public humiliation brings.)

Generally, the more public speaking you do, the less nervous you will become. So do it a lot. Unfamiliar situations make us nervous. The most nervous I have ever been for a public speaking performance was the first time I did stand-up comedy. I was nervous for about a week beforehand. The second time I did it I was only nervous for about four days. The time after that, only for two days. The more I did it the less nervous I got, and the shorter the time I got nervous for. The 227th time I did it I was nervous for only about 20 minutes. The more exposure you get to public speaking the more in control you will feel. With experience you will better be able to anticipate the problems that may arise and have strategies for dealing with them, and you will know that when things do go horribly wrong it's not the end of the world. Whether you consciously analyse your performance or not, every time you do some public speaking you will learn something. Especially when it doesn't go well.

Now let's get specific.

Firstly, find out what you do when you are nervous. Next time you're nervous, do a mental audit of what you are doing. Are your hands shaking? Are you pacing up and down? Fidgeting? Chewing your nails? Screaming? What are you thinking about? How does your voice sound? Are you breathing faster than normal?

If you address the *symptoms* your nervousness is producing, before you know it the feeling that is producing those symptoms, that is the nervousness itself, is likely to diminish, too.

If you tell yourself to stop feeling nervous, it is unlikely to have any effect. But if you tell yourself to stop fidgeting, it is a relatively easy command to follow. Look down at your hands twisting themselves into scared knots, and tell them to stop. Rest them calmly in your lap. You'll immediately want to start fidgeting again. Don't. Then tell yourself to stop pacing up and down. That's pretty easy to do too. Just sit down. Then tell yourself to breathe deeply and gently. Finally, tell yourself to stop screaming. Then go back and check if you have started to fidget again. You probably have. Gently make yourself stop again. Then re-check the rest of your symptoms. Keep going until you have made yourself *look* as if you are just sitting calmly. If you can successfully control the physical signs nervousness produces, before you know it, it's likely that you will *feel* calmer as well.

Having done that, you now know the things you do when you are nervous. And, one by one you can stop doing those things.

Nerves generally make you feel as if everything is speeding up. The adrenalin makes us want to rush. So slow down. Do everything a little bit more slowly and deliberately than you would normally. Be aware of all your movements. If I notice I am pacing rapidly I make myself sit still. And if I then have to get up and go somewhere, I make sure that I stroll as languidly and lazily as anyone has ever strolled.

I make whatever I do deliberate because I know that soon I am going to have to convince an audience that I am utterly in control and utterly comfortable. So I try to start projecting that illusion before I go on. I try to act as though I am totally in control, as though I own the room. Someone who owns the room never hurries, they look relaxed.

I don't feel in control, I don't feel relaxed, but I make myself act as if I do. And you know what? Before I know it, my relaxed body has conned my anxious mind, and the fact that I am *acting* relaxed actually begins to make me *feel* relaxed. If you can control your outward manifestations of nerves, in all likelihood you will soon feel calmer inside as well.

When I started doing stand-up comedy, every night I was on I would be terrified. One night just before I went on I was scuttling from backstage to the toilet and on the way I bumped into two people and tripped over a chair. Nerves. I was rushing for no reason and not paying any attention to where I was going.

From then on, whenever I caught myself hurrying before a gig I would slow down, and consciously adopt an utterly relaxed lazy slow stroll. Before too long people were commenting on how relaxed I was. Of course I wasn't relaxed at all. I was just walking slower, but the fact that I did slow down actually helped me become more aware of everything that was going on around me. I was less caught up in my frantic mind, and more involved in my immediate environment, which is exactly how you want to be when you go on stage. On stage you need to be utterly in the moment. You need to be aware of, and process, everything that is going on.

The fact that people tell me I look relaxed becomes self-fulfilling. If people tell you that you look cool, it makes you feel cool. Before too long I started to believe that nerves just weren't a problem. And soon after that they rarely were.

There's another good reason for slowing yourself down. People talk about how time rushes on stage and how everything seems to happen quickly. If you go on stage with your heart pounding, and breathing shallowly after having spent the last hour fidgeting, bumping into things and talking too quickly, of course things are going to happen too quickly. If you've been rushing inside your head off stage, you'll keep rushing once you go on. If you want to be centred and in control on stage, you need to be centred and in control before you go on.

That covers the physical effects of nerves, but how can you control their psychological effects? As I've just said, controlling the physical effects will help. By acting relaxed, the body can con the mind. But your state of mind when you go on stage is vital. If you start off feeling flustered and all over the place, it's hard to recover. But if you start strong, confident and in control, that confidence will build on itself and soon you'll be flying.

The ideal state of mind just before you go on stage is the state of mind you want to be in when you are on stage. And that is to be utterly in the moment, to be utterly aware of what is happening right now, rather than thinking about what just happened or what is about to happen. Think of the last time you were engaged in something that took your complete concentration. It could have been rock-climbing, squash, childbirth, sex, a stimulating conversation, sitting an exam, work, surfing or reading a book. Remember that feeling of total absorption. You were totally aware of what was happening in the present. Your mind wasn't drifting off to worry about that bill you forget to pay yesterday or to wonder how that important meeting would go tomorrow, because its full capacity was needed right here and now to help you concentrate completely on the task at hand. That state of mind is the exact opposite of being bored, and it allows you to be fully involved in whatever it is you are doing.

That's the best state to be in when you go on stage. However, the overwhelming temptation when you are nervous is to think about the thing you are nervous about. So if before a talk you are nervous, it is likely you will be thinking about your talk, running through your lines and thinking about how best to deliver them. This can be useful, in that some of the most effective preparation is done at the last minute. But too much of it can be counterproductive. When you are nervous, you don't tend to calmly run through the main points you are going to make and think about how you are going to make them. Rather, you tend to fantasise about forgetting what you are going to say, or getting tongue-tied, and how disastrous it's going to be when things go wrong.

Prepare your talk thoroughly, so you don't need to do a last-minute cram. Then before you go on, wherever you are, just concentrate on what is happening now. Look around, listen, try to focus all your awareness on what is going on. Why? Firstly, you are bringing yourself into the moment, and that is where you need to be when you give your talk. Secondly, you are distracting yourself from all the terrifying thoughts of failure you are probably having. And thirdly, you may well see something or hear something that will be of use in your talk. Often, and I'll write more about this later, if you keep your eyes and ears open in the hour before your talk you will be presented with the perfect ice-breaker to create an immediate sense of connection with your audience.

> Find somewhere to sit quietly, where you have a good view of what's going on. If your talk is one of several happenings, sit in the audience and soak up the vibe for a while. You'll get a sense of the mood of the room, and how people are reacting. Try to sit at the back or to one side so if you want to step out and look at your notes or go for a walk you can.

If your speech is written down you may want to look over it a couple of times. That makes sense but make sure that what you do is productive. If you spend too long looking through your notes you will probably end up just looking, not seeing. All that you will really be doing is trying to reassure yourself that everything will be all right by doing something. If you find yourself mindlessly looking at your notes without really taking anything in, then well done, at least you've realised you are doing it. Get up and go for a walk, preferably outside in the fresh air. Clear your head. In fact whenever you feel your nervousness getting out of control, a walk can be a great help. It allows you to burn some of the adrenalin pumping around your body, it's something most of us find relaxing (unless it's up a mountain carrying a stove) and a change of physical environment can help break the patterns your mind is getting itself hooked on. But don't stride out too far or too fast. The adrenalin you are burning is there for a reason; it's to give you energy and awareness on stage, so don't exhaust yourself. While you are walking, try to concentrate on what you see and hear and smell. Be in the moment.

So when you look at your notes, focus and really apply your concentration to them for a specific time. Concentrate hard, start at the beginning, go right through to the end—and then stop. Doing this may give you some new ideas for your speech, or help you think of a better way of saying something. Trust yourself to make these changes. You have never known as much about the subject you are about to speak on as in the moments just before you give your speech.

Just before you go on

It's important to have some exposure to your audience before you go on. If there are speakers before you, try to sit at the back of the audience for a while and listen. What is working? What isn't? Does the audience seem to have a sense of humour? Who are they? Are they old? Young? Tired? Sober? Drunk? Are there any in-jokes you can pick up on? Has a previous speaker said anything that you can turn into an ice-breaker, a funny comment? Even when you are the first speaker you can still try to get a look at the audience as they come in. The more you know about them the better.

If you're doing your speech during or after a lunch or a dinner it's a good idea to get yourself seated among them, share the meal and find out more about them and the vibe. In my experience this is almost guaranteed to give you something you can use in your speech. What's the alternative? Pacing up and down some dingy dressing room, or more likely corridor, wondering what the audience is like. Sit down with them and find out. At the very least it will help you relax. The other guests will almost always be nice to you, and you can pump them for information. Sometimes what you pick up will be vital, and may even save your speech.

I was once booked to give an after-dinner speech to a group of lawyers at a conference. I prepared half an hour of funny stuff based on my time as a lawyer, but also branching out into general funny stuff. A tailored stand-up comedy routine.

During dinner, I asked who they had had as speakers in previous years (always a good thing to do). Two people who I imagined would have given pretty serious talks were mentioned— and I sort of twigged that they had been low on gags and big on ideas. I also sensed the expectation that there would be some meat in my speech. I didn't have any, so I had to get some fast. But how? Several people at my table were talking about the difficulty of getting the balance between work and the rest of their life right. I knew from my own experience in corporate law that the culture often demands long hours at the office, and I surmised that work–life balance was probably an issue for many there. It's also something I care a lot about, so between bites of my chicken I tried to think through some ideas and jot down some notes.

When it was time to speak, I started off with the funny stuff as I had planned, but toward the end I slowed down, stood still and talked seriously about how important it was for everyone to make sure they got the balance right between their work and the rest of their life, because if they didn't, then some time in the future, when it was too late they'd realise they'd missed out on a lot. It turned out to be pitched just right. Work–life balance was an issue many in the audience were struggling with. Had I been pacing about backstage or too focused on what I was going to say I would have missed the hints and delivered the wrong speech.

Very often a lunch or dinner function will be running late, and the organisers may well tell you it's time to go on while people are still eating or plates are cleared. Resist. Take control of the situation. Suggest you wait. If they insist, remind them of the agreement you made that you wouldn't speak during eating time.

The first few minutes of your speech are the most important, and if there is a high level of distraction at that time you will pay the price for the entire speech.

Make sure you have a full glass of water nearby when you are speaking. It is very common to get a dry mouth when you are nervous and when there is no water handy it can feel as if every word you say is covered in dust.

Being introduced

If you are getting an introduction, make sure you talk to the person who will be doing it. Be nice. If they like you they'll give you a better introduction, so have a good chat with them.

Ask how the person is going to introduce you, and check that it's brief and relevant. A long intro is embarrassing. Worse, if you get built up too much, it's just a further distance to fall. Ask your introducer to remind people to turn off their phones.

If people are seated around tables so that some of them have their backs to the stage, ask the person introducing you to get them to turn their chairs around. It's hard to pay attention to someone if your neck is craned around 180 degrees.

Notes

Most speaking situations are set up so that you can use notes if you want them. That usually means you speak from a lectern. Whether or not there is a lectern or something else that makes it possible to use notes is one of things you need to find out before you give your speech.

With a lectern in front of you, no one can see your notes so they forget you are using them. Holding notes without the protection of a lectern generally looks messy, and it's a continual reminder to the audience that you are not talking to them, you are 'giving a speech'. It makes it less intimate. It's also clumsy and awkward to be holding notes with nothing to rest them on, especially if you have a microphone in the other hand.

Ideally, you will know your subject matter so well that you don't need your speech written out in front of you to remind you of what you are going to say. You should be in the position where you can trust your knowledge to such an extent that you know you can talk freely about your subject.

Having said that, it's great to have notes. Knowing that you have everything you want to say written down in front of you creates a great feeling of security and confidence and eliminates one of the most common fears of public speaking—that you will forget what you were going to say. Working from written notes also means you don't have to spend a lot of time *memorising* by rote what you are going to say. Instead you can spend that time *thinking* about what you are going to say and how you are going to say it.

I often type out my whole speech word for word. If you have worked hard on getting the wording of your speech right, you may as well take advantage of that work and have the precise wording down in front of you.

However, if you do have your speech written out word for word, there are a couple of things to avoid. Remember you are not there to read. You are there to talk to people. You need to look people in the eye and engage them—and you can't do that if your head is buried in notes. So practise looking down at your speech, then up at the audience, down then up, down then up. If your preparation has been good you shouldn't need to look at every word anyway. A glance at the first few words of a paragraph will usually be enough to set you on your way.

As well as engaging physically with the audience by making eye contact, you need to engage with them verbally. Don't let the fact that your speech is typed out in front of you be an excuse to lapse into a dull monotone. Invest your words with emotion and meaning. The speech is not the words written on the page, it is what is in your head and your heart.

Don't let yourself be trapped by the written word. We've talked about writing your speech out in the language in which you talk, rather than the language in which you write. No matter how conscientiously you try to do that, there will often be moments when you want to say something in a different way to the way you have written it. Don't feel that you are tied to your typescript. Say what feels right at the time. Come back to the written word if and when you need to.

While I often type out my speech word for word, I rarely stick religiously to what I have typed. I follow the structure, and use it as a reminder of the things I want to talk about, and to make sure I don't skip something important, but usually the words I need will come without it. When I have done enough preparation and I know what I am talking about, then I will be able to talk about it. If I have written a joke that requires precise delivery, then I might return to the page to ensure I get it right, but usually the written speech will be more of a guideline than an exact replica of what I say.

You may prefer to talk simply from a series of points. You may have just eight words written on a scrap of paper. If that is all you feel you need to remind you of the points you want to make, great.

As you walk on, hold your notes on the side of your body away from the audience. If you are walking on with your right shoulder to the audience, carry your notes in your left hand. Why? It's not necessarily a case of disguising that you have notes, it's more a matter of ensuring that one of the first things the audience thinks when they see you is not, 'Hey. Look. He's got notes'. You want them to think you've come to talk to them, not that you've come to read a speech to them. So don't flap your notes around.

If you want to do stand-up comedy, forget notes. You have to memorise the lot!

four
TALKING

How do I start?

So finally the moment has arrived. You're on. How do you start? Let's begin with a couple of don'ts.

Don't start with a long list of welcomes

Whoever you are and whatever you are talking about, as you walk out to face your audience you face a moment of expectation. 'Who is this?' 'What are they going to be like?' 'Are they going to be worth listening to?' And most importantly, 'Will they be boring?' The audience wants to know the answers. And if the first thing you say is, 'Ladies and gentlemen, distinguished guests, managing director, vice chairman of the advisory committee, deputy director of the administrative board and acting deputy head of the steering committee', you will have answered all those questions in one hit. And the answers you will have given will be:

- 'Who is this?' Someone who sounds just like everyone else we get at these things.
- 'What are they going to be like?' Dull.
- 'Is he going to be worth listening to?' No.
- 'Will he be boring?' Yes.

In the first minute of your talk everyone is listening hard to work out what you will be like. Don't waste that attention.

Don't summarise what you are going to say at the start of your talk

Each time I hear someone say 'in this talk I will do this, then I will do that, then finally I will discuss this', I cringe. How can you expect an audience to hang on your every word when they know what is going to happen? We talked earlier about creating tension. There is tension at the start of every talk because people want to know what is going to happen. If you tell them what's going to happen, you immediately eliminate it.

Imagine if your parents had summarised at the beginning of *Jack and the Beanstalk*:

> In this story I will explain how Jack found a magic bean that grew into a huge tree and how at the top of the tree he found a terrifying giant who almost ate him up. Then I will tell you how Jack escaped and all ended well.

Not much point listening once you know that.

If you summarise what you're going to say, you remove the most important reason people have for listening—the desire to know what happens next. Don't spoil the surprise. Use it to maintain tension and to keep them interested.

The first couple of minutes are the most important of any speech. Within that time people have assessed whether they think you are worth listening to, and if they've made that assessment in the negative it's hard to get them to change their minds. It's not impossible, you can recover from a bad start, but if you can start well it's a huge advantage.

The first thing you say should be something natural. Something you'd say if you'd just been introduced to someone at a party—'hello', 'hi', or whatever you normally say. If they have applauded your entrance you might want to say 'thanks'. If they haven't applauded you might want to say 'thanks' with a touch of sarcasm to try for a laugh, but do it with a smile so they don't think you're a grump.

Ideally, at the start of a speech you should do two things that might seem contradictory. The first is to build a bridge of connection to the audience. Give them an opportunity to think, 'Hey, he's just a regular person like me.' If you can do this you will build up a sense of empathy, and your audience will be more willing to come along on the journey you are about to take them on.

The second thing is to make the audience think you are worthy of their attention and respect. That in fact you're not just a regular person like them; that you are someone who has particular insights, knowledge, jokes or something else worth listening to.

So on one hand you need to tell your audience that you're just like them, while on the other hand you need to tell them that you are a bit cleverer or more insightful or more knowledgeable or funnier than they are so that they will want to listen to you. Here's how you do it.

The most clichéd opening line in the world is: 'A funny thing happened to me on the way here tonight'. The reason it has been used so much is that it does both the things I'm talking about. It both builds a bridge to the audience, and lets them know the speaker is worth listening to. It does this by referring to something that the speaker and everyone in the audience has in common—that is, they have all travelled to the place where they are now. Everyone who is there got there somehow. So by saying, 'A funny thing happened to me on the way here tonight,' the speaker is immediately communicating that he is just like them, that he shares an experience with all of them.

Then the speaker tells the audience what the funny thing that happened to him on the way here tonight was, and of course it's something funny. That sends a message to the audience that although the speaker is someone who, just like them, had to travel here tonight, he had the cleverness and the wit to observe something hilarious that happened along the way. 'Gee,' the audience thinks, 'I travelled here tonight, too, and I didn't see anything funny. Gosh,' they think, 'if he was able to observe something funny just on the way here tonight, he must be pretty clever and pretty observant. And pretty funny. I bet he's going to be really clever and observant and funny when he really gets into his speech. I don't want to miss that.' You have got them where you want them. You have made a connection, and also given them a reason to listen to what you have to say.

Mission accomplished. Of course, no one will think all those things consciously. Hopefully, they'll be too busy laughing. But at a subconscious level, those will be the messages that are being communicated.

Ice-breakers

You could describe an opening line like 'A funny thing happened on the way here tonight' as an ice-breaker, and the right ice-breaker is a fantastic way of sending out the two messages that you are just like your audience, but that you are also special enough to be worth listening to. An ice-breaker is often at least mildly humorous, and ideally it's something that sounds off the cuff (even if it's not), as if it's just something that, by the way, you want to mention before you start. Sometimes when I do stand-up comedy I begin by saying, 'Before I start I just want to tell you about this thing I saw today'. Then I tell them about whatever it was. It doesn't have to be hilarious, because what it's doing is immediately communicating to the audience that I'm not there to do an 'act' for them, I'm there to talk to them, person to person. If you sound spontaneous and fresh, particularly if you can find a way to show them that you are somehow one of them in the process, the audience will want to listen to you.

The second purpose of an ice-breaker is to subtly communicate that you are not just there to recite something you wrote a week ago, but that you are involved, present and aware of exactly what is happening right here and right now, that you are a person well worth listening to because you are entertaining, funny and smart. All that in one line. You want to form a connection with them, but you also want them to respect you.

The best ice-breakers don't sound as if they're part of a speech at all. Here are a few. But one proviso: if you use any of them yourself, you're sort of missing the point. Being a good speech-maker isn't about collecting clever sayings and witty remarks from others' bowerbird style, then pretending they're your own. It's about developing the skills to write and deliver a good speech for yourself, including the opening.

A good ice-breaker can comment on where you are

Before I start, has anyone else noticed that if you look up at the roof it looks exactly like that spaceship in Close Encounters of the Third Kind*?*

The message: 'I'm just like you, I'm here . . . but I'm slightly more observant than you'.

I once made a speech at the anniversary of the opening of a library. There was a crowd of about 50 well-dressed library fans, most of them over forty, standing in front of where I was speaking. Between them and me someone had placed a couple of portable crowd dividers. So my opening line was:

Hello, it's nice to be here and can I first say, thank goodness for these crowd barriers. You look like a pretty out of control bunch, we're in a pretty wild environment, and obviously things could easily get out of hand tonight. It makes me a feel a lot safer to know that if you do all go berserk and rush the stage, I'll be protected.

Maybe you can make a comment about the strange shape of the room you are in, or about a painting or some other feature in it. It just needs to be a little observation that proves to the audience you are capable of doing more than pulling out a speech and reading it.

Say what everyone is thinking

If there is a noisy airconditioner, for example, don't ignore it, acknowledge it:

Good evening. It's nice to be here but I must say I've never been heckled by an airconditioner before.

I once did a gig in the middle of a rainforest north of Cairns. We had all been driven 45 minutes through the dark to get there. So my opening line was,

> *Hello, it's great to be here . . . wherever the hell we are.*

It worked because everyone had been thinking, 'What a lovely place, but where are we?'

Give voice to what everyone else is thinking, and you will have a perfect ice-breaker.

A good ice-breaker can comment on something that has happened earlier

> *Thanks, and can I just say how sorry I am I wasn't here for the previous session on economic responsibility in marketplace reserve interest trends. Obviously I can't hope to be as entertaining as a session on that, but I'll do my best.*

A good ice-breaker can comment on who the audience are

> *It's very nice to be here talking to a group of lawyers, but before I start let me get one thing straight. Last time I spoke to one lawyer for half an hour it cost me a hundred bucks. So if I'm speaking for half an hour and there are 120 of you here today, how much is this going to cost me?*

The perfect ice-breaker can come from the circumstances in which you are asked to speak

Imagine being asked to give a funny speech about a very serious topic. You could begin by saying:

When they rang me to do this talk they said, 'We're running a conference on separation and divorce. It's a very sensitive subject and there's often a fair bit of tension. We want you to give a funny speech on separation, divorce and family law issues that doesn't offend anyone.' I said, 'Gee, that should be easy. Thanks a lot.'

That would be a great opening line because it would acknowledge all the tension in the room, and make everyone there see things from a totally different angle. Yes, they did have many serious, complex and sensitive issues to discuss, but what about the poor speaker who had to try to make them all laugh about it?

Look and listen

If you keep your ears and eyes open, it's amazing how often you'll see or hear something in the half hour before your speech that you can use as your ice-breaker.

I spoke at a conference that had a lot to do with gender roles and how they were changing, and on the way to the toilet just before I went on I heard a woman in the foyer on her mobile phone talking to what must have been her husband or partner, and saying, 'No, I *haven't* just been running around shopping all day. It's a proper conference.' All I had to do was comment on what the conference was about, repeat the conversation and tell them that maybe we all still had a way to go.

Once at a work function where I was speaking I was in the toilets when I heard someone say to his mate, 'I'm at the table with all the bosses. And some comedian I've never heard of. It's so boring.' He was, of course sitting at the same table as I was, and again all I had to do was repeat what I had heard to get the perfect ice-breaker.

I spoke to the partners of a law firm away on a group weekend. When I was briefed I was told, 'This group is probably the wildest bunch of law partners you will ever see.' When I started I told them what I had been told and made fun of the fact that law partners don't exactly have a reputation for wildness, so the fact that they were the wildest bunch around meant what? That they'd be up to half-past ten?

You may even get an ice-breaker from the person who introduces you. If they waffle on for a long time, when you come on you can say, 'Thank you, and after we deduct the time that introduction took from the time I've been given to speak, I guess I've got about three minutes left'.

A speaker is very often an outsider. Members of the audience will usually have more in common with each other than they do with you as, for example, when they are all from a company or an industry that you aren't a member of. Part of the briefing process is for you to gain information that will help you appear to be more of an insider than you are, but sometimes you can create an ice-breaker from the very fact that you are an outsider. For example:

> *I was listening carefully to what John was saying about fixed ratio interest-bearing deposits, and I had no idea what he was talking about. I'm sorry, it made no sense to me at all.*

It's a fair bet that anything that strikes you as noteworthy or interesting or unusual will strike everyone else who saw it or heard it or smelt it as noteworthy or interesting or unusual too. So use those things.

Presentation

Having put all that hard work into preparing a speech and ensuring that the conditions are as good as they can be for you to deliver it, how do you make sure that when you actually stand up and start talking it all comes out as well as it can?

The first thing is to make sure you're thoroughly prepared. The better prepared you are the better the chances it will go well on the day. When you've prepared well, a disaster is very unlikely.

Remember standing outside the exam room about to go in? You felt as if your whole future would be determined by what happened in the next couple of hours. But you were wrong. In fact, the major determinant of how well you performed in the exam was how well you had prepared. If you had done enough study it would have been hard to fail, and if you hadn't done enough study it would have been hard to pass.

Having said that, how well you perform is still a big factor in how well your speech is received. I say 'perform' and I mean 'perform'. The most entertaining, hilarious and informative content in the world can be killed by poor presentation, just as the driest, dullest subject matter can be brought to life by a good presentation.

Now you may be thinking to yourself that you aren't a performer. It doesn't matter. I'm not talking about putting on make-up and playing Hamlet. What I am talking about is being able to deliver your speech in the best way possible. That is, to speak with emotion, emphasis, excitement and passion.

> There are lots of little things to learn about delivering a speech, but the simplest and most important is this: believe in what you say and believe that it is important. Make it matter to you and then it will matter to those listening.

Having researched and written your speech and gone over it again and again, by the time you get to deliver it you may well be a bit over it. Well, too bad. To get the audience interested you need to be interested. Tell yourself that this is your one chance to tell people all the important things you spent all that time researching and preparing. Make it matter.

Be present

If you've ever seen a stand-up comedian you enjoyed, you probably believed they were telling you things that they had just thought of, that they were sharing their spontaneous observations of the world with you in a way they had never done before. If you did, well, I hate to tell you, but in the great majority of cases you would have been wrong. Most comedians gradually build up an act over months and years and the jokes that sounded so spontaneous may well have been delivered hundreds of times before to different crowds. The skill lies in thinking of them in the first place, then ensuring that every time they are delivered they sound fresh and spontaneous. A stand-up comedian, or a public speaker, who sounds as if they are just reciting a script, is gone.

As far as I can work out, the more in the moment I am on stage, the better my performance is. Ideally I won't be thinking about the future (What will happen if I can't remember the next thing I have to say? Is my speech going okay?) or the past (Why did I stumble over that word? Why didn't that last line get a bigger laugh?). Ideally I will just be concentrating on doing my job. I won't be thinking about giving my speech. I will just be giving it. I will be totally involved in giving my speech.

All sorts of unexpected things can happen to you when you are public speaking, but if you get in the moment and completely involve yourself in doing your job you'll surprise yourself at how well you react to the unexpected. The brain is a fine instrument and if you get out of its way and let it do its work, it can come up with some amazing things.

How do you get in the moment? A lot of it is about feeling relaxed and at home on stage. To some extent, that will only come with time. Always make yourself familiar with the physical layout of the stage and the room. If you have stomped about on it beforehand you will feel a bit more comfortable when you get up there.

You can't expect to switch mental states as you walk on stage. It's very hard to go from thinking totally about something that will happen in the future (that is, your speech) while you are backstage to being completely alive and in the moment the moment you walk on stage. So in those moments before you go on, bring yourself into the moment. Listen. What do you hear? Look. What do you see? What does the chair you are sitting on feel like? Can you smell anything? Your senses bring you into the moment. Use them.

If you have written a decent speech and you know what you are going to say, and you are in the right space mentally, if you are focused on what you are doing right now, and you have used the time immediately preceding the speech to gain some insights that will help you connect to the audience, then you are in a perfect position to deliver a good speech.

Although content is important, an audience often decides whether or not a speaker deserves to be listened to very quickly, before they have really had a chance to assess the worth of your content. They assess—and this is often a subconscious process—the manner of the speaker, the way they speak and their body language.

Good speakers command attention. The ability to command attention comes largely from confidence, and true confidence usually comes from experience and preparation. Nevertheless, you can learn to fake confidence. If you look confident, if you exude confidence to the audience, the battle is half won. That doesn't mean you can't be scared or insecure. It just means you can't show that you are scared and insecure.

You need to give the audience the impression that you are utterly at home on the stage. You need to be natural. You need to be yourself. Ignore thoughts of a stage persona. Be who you are. Good public speakers are natural. They are genuine. Except for this—ideally, on stage you probably want to be a slightly heightened version of yourself. That is, to be a bit more confident, a bit more extroverted and a bit more enthusiastic than you normally are.

Connect

Speeches, like conversation, work when there is a sense of personal connection. You need to make those listening feel that you are talking to them and with them, not at them, and you do that in the same way you establish a sense of personal connection in a conversation.

Firstly, make eye contact. Obviously if there are 150 people in your audience it's going to be hard to look them all deeply in the eye, but they understand that. Look up and out at them. Make sure that you regularly look at each section of the audience. I mentioned earlier how important it is to have clear sightlines to everyone. If they can't see you it's very hard to connect with them, and therefore very hard to get them to listen. If you never look at your audience, if you stare down and read your speech, then they may as well all be behind a pillar. That's a major reason why you should be familiar with your speech—so you don't have to keep looking down at it. Look at *them*.

Don't fall into the trap of looking just at the part of the audience that's in front of you. If there are some to your right, some in front of you and others to your left, look up and out to them all. Mix it up. For example, look at your notes, look at those in front of you, look at your notes, look at those on your right, look at your notes, look at those on your left, and so on. Spend most time looking at the part of the audience where there are most people. Sometimes you may have a light in your eyes that is so bright that you can't actually see the audience. Look up and out anyway. It's not about you seeing them; it's about them seeing you. Look out at where they are as if you can see them. Don't put your hand up to block the light or try to step out of it. The light is there so that they can see you. It helps focus the audience's attention on you. So get used to it.

Be anchored. Stand still and strong in the middle of the stage. If you have a lectern that's easy. Stand behind it. One theory is that lecterns were invented to give speakers something to hold onto to stop them collapsing. If you don't have a lectern, find a base to talk from. You can move around if it feels natural, but that can be distracting. It can also make you look nervous. But the most important thing is that you feel natural and not artificial. If walking around and around in circles on the stage feels natural to you, then it's good. As a general rule anything that feels natural will do two things, both of them good. It will help you relax and it will make you look relaxed. The more relaxed you feel the better you will perform, and the more relaxed you look, the more relaxed and receptive the audience will be. But before you take this as a licence to pace, work out whether pacing is really something you do naturally, or whether it's just nerves making you want to do it. Generally it's easier for an audience to look at a fixed point. If you are pacing in circles while you speak they might get dizzy. So might you.

The other advantage of at least beginning your speech standing still is that then when you do move or gesture it means something. You can use gestures and movement to emphasise something important. If you start your speech moving all over the place, then you have nothing extra to rise to when you want to emphasise something important. However, don't over-think this. Generally it's more important to be natural than it is to do something that feels unnatural because you read in a book it was a good idea.

Be natural

Speak like you speak. Talk like you are having a conversation with someone, not like you are delivering a speech. People respond well to a conversational approach, they are used to it. Generally they don't like to be lectured. A lecture is didactic; it implies that a captive audience is having information imposed upon it. Even if that is what you are trying to do, you don't want to give the impression of it. The more conversational and natural your speaking style, the more it sends a message that this is a conversation and not a lecture, and the more receptive your audience will be.

A good trick to help you get into this style is to pretend you are answering questions. Try this. Imagine you are giving a one-minute talk on how to make a salad. Do it now in your head. Describe in one minute how to make a salad.

Once you have done that, imagine you are at a party and someone asks you the question, 'How do you make a salad?' How would you answer? Answer the question now. Now compare the two versions. The second was probably a lot less formal and more conversational than the first, and probably more eloquent. In all likelihood it would have connected better with a listener because, instead of talking as if you were giving a speech, you were just talking. So, if you are giving a speech on the mechanical dynamics of the internal combustion engine, say, just before you go on imagine that someone has just asked you, 'How do the mechanical dynamics of the internal combustion engine work?' Then go out there and simply answer the question.

Speak like you speak. Some people think that when they give a speech they have to speak as if they are giving a speech: slowly, with long pauses, and in an unnatural, stylised way. Don't think of it as public speaking, think of it as speaking.

A good way to illustrate the difference between the artificial 'giving a speech' type of speaking and normal speaking is to watch someone giving a speech and to observe the difference between the way they speak when they are giving the speech proper, and the way they speak when they are answering questions at the end.

With a good public speaker there will be very little difference. But with many there will be a marked change between the formal, artificial rhythms and delivery of the speech and the natural way of phrasing things they use when they are responding to questions.

> You should speak like you do in normal speech, using the same language, rhythms and words. A speech is simply a conversation where you just happen to be doing all the talking. A speech is just like talking to one person, except there are actually lots of them.

What if you are reading your speech? Surely it is impossible to make it sound natural. Not necessarily. Some people are very good at reading in their natural speaking voice. If you have written your speech so that it sounds like the way you talk, then it's perfectly possible to read it and still sound conversational—as long as you remember that you are speaking and not reading.

Usually, having the speech all written out in front of us is more of a security blanket than something we actually need. If the pages blew away, we could still give our speech. When I have a word-for-word speech written out, all I normally do is look down, see a word or two and think, 'Oh yes, this is the bit about eggs', look back up again and talk about the eggs. If I have prepared properly, it's all in my head. I know it. And if I ever get lost or lose eloquence, I can just return to the page for a while.

Pace

Another common problem is speaking too quickly. This comes from nerves. When you speak too fast it's difficult for people to take in everything you are saying. Even if they understand all the words, the pace the information is coming at them may just be too great. When you lose the ability to emphasise particular phrases and to texture your words, all the audience hears is an unstoppable torrent of words, and soon they all sound the same and become meaningless. Plus, if you're speaking fast you may just as well come out carrying a big sign with the words, 'Hi. I'm nervous', written on it.

The solution is obvious. Slow down. But it's easier said than done. Try this. Firstly, before you go on try to identify how nervous you are. If you are nervous, be aware that one effect may well be that you will race through your speech too quickly. Do what you can to settle yourself before you start. Breathe deeply and concentrate on what's happening now. When you go on, take a moment and look out at the audience. Take a deep breath, smile and say 'Hello', just as you would to someone you've just been introduced to. For the first few minutes concentrate on connecting with your audience. Emphasise the words you are saying. They are important words that you have agonised over, and each one needs to be parcelled up and delivered to the audience by your voice in exactly the right way.

Don't overdo the slowing-down thing. I'm not suggesting you dawdle through a speech without energy. A good speech needs pace and power behind the words. You need to channel the energy that nervousness provides you with, rather than wasting it by ripping up beer coasters backstage and then hurtling through your speech as fast as you can.

What a speaker often feels when they are nervous is that they are losing the audience. The temptation then is to rush on faster and faster. Don't do it. The faster you go, the quicker you'll lose them. Trust the words you have written, respect them and give the audience the opportunity to hear them. Slow down, make each word deliberate and concentrate on investing your words with the meaning and importance they deserve.

Mistakes

Be human. If you make a mistake, acknowledge it. We all mispronounce words or fluff sentences from time to time, and we are particularly likely to do it when public speaking because of the pressure involved. What matters is not the fact that you have made a mistake, but how you react to it. Remember this. If you obviously stumble, everyone will notice it. Remember also that a good way to connect when public speaking is to say what everyone is thinking. So if you make a mistake, acknowledge it. If you were going to say 'behind the shed', then changed your mind and decided to say 'around the back of the shed', but then it actually came out of your mouth as 'around the behind of the shed', acknowledge the mistake and have a laugh about it.

Mistakes are not disasters. They are opportunities for you to show the audience that you are not a scared robot, but a real person who doesn't take themselves too seriously. Explain what you were trying to say and why it came out wrong. If you can laugh at yourself for making a mistake the audience will see it as a sign of real self-confidence. Anything that changes the dynamic of a speech is interesting, at least initially. If you react humanly to making a mistake it can relieve tension, give the audience a quick break or remind them that what they are listening to isn't a perfectly scripted metronomic performance, it's a human being.

Using your voice

How important is the sound of your voice? Some people, through no effort of their own, are born with great speaking voices. Others, most of us, aren't. A great speaking voice is deep, resonant and powerful. It projects authority. I don't know why we seem to respect a deep voice, but in my experience we do. I do not have a naturally good speaking voice. It's definitely not deep or resonant. But I don't think it matters much. What's more important is what you do with your voice.

I'm not a big fan of classes that teach you to speak properly. I believe that the most valuable thing you have to offer as a speaker is yourself: you as you are, speaking naturally, not you with all your edges knocked off. However, if you want to take voice classes, give it a go and decide for yourself.

> Whatever type of voice you have, what you do with it is more important than what it sounds like. Using variations in pace, emphasis and volume can make a huge difference to your speech.

Very few great speeches have been given by someone whispering softly into a microphone, however. The sound of a voice raised and powerful, full of passion and power, is capable almost on its own of creating excitement in an audience. There was nothing quietly spoken about the great speeches of Martin Luther King and John F. Kennedy.

I don't mean you should shout the whole thing. What is important is to learn how to use your voice to complement the content of what you are saying. A monotone is dull because it's all the same. Speaking at the same pitch, pace and volume all through your speech is like driving a manual car and not using the gears. You'll still get there, but not in nearly as much comfort or style.

These are some of the ways you can use your voice:

- Use it to build up to something. If you are trying to excite someone about a new idea or project you can, as you describe it, gradually increase the pace and volume of what you are saying, thereby building an atmosphere of gradually increasing excitement. If you want them to get excited, get excited yourself. If the audience hears the excitement building in your voice, it will excite them.
- Use emphasis. If you want to emphasise a particular key point, slow down, and say each word of it loudly, slowly and carefully. Then you might want to repeat it.

  Don't be afraid to flag that something important is coming. If you tell people something you think is important is coming up it gives them a chance to focus in on what it is. For example:

  The most important thing I want to say to you is this. (PAUSE . . . then clearly and slowly) The best way of cooking potatoes is to boil them. (PAUSE) The best way of cooking them is to boil them.

Now that may look daggy in print, but if you say it with belief and conviction it will work.

If you are saying something that you think is important, say it like it *is* important. If it's a key message of your speech, don't just say it like any old sentence. Say it with emphasis and conviction and belief. Usually that means saying it more loudly and slowly, and perhaps with a deeper tone of voice.

If you are saying something you think is important, don't be afraid to repeat it. Say it once. Then pause to let them take it in. Then say it again.

- If you want to build tension, slowly lower your volume. Gradually speak softer and softer. Bring them in. It's a wonderful feeling to actually see almost everyone in an audience literally leaning forward to catch your every word.

You can build your speech into waves, building gradually to points where you speak loudly with passion and power, and your body and gestures are animated, and then returning to a less forceful, more measured tone until you again build up to make your next point. Say you wanted to make six points in your speech. For the first point, lay the groundwork in a controlled and restrained manner, giving the facts in clear, functional language. As you build your case and head toward the conclusion that will drive home the point you want to make, start to let rip. Get louder and more passionate. Speak like you care. Don't be afraid to get fired up, don't be afraid to hit the lectern with your fist and don't be afraid to raise your voice. Speak like it matters, show you care. Make your conclusion count. Then move on to your second point and again lay the groundwork in a controlled, restrained manner.

You can't hit the lectern and shout for a whole half an hour. Your audience will get sick of it, and your hand will get sore, so pick the points at which passion is going to be most appropriate and will best complement what you are saying, and pick other points where clear logical analysis is needed. The more contrast and variety you use, the easier it will be to keep the audience's attention.

Remember the tiger example?

> *I was creeping through the jungle then I saw a tiger in front of me. Then I heard a noise to my left. There was another tiger. And another. Then there was a roar behind me. I turned around and there two more tigers! I was surrounded by five tigers! Can you imagine being surrounded by five tigers? Can you imagine how scared I was? I was terrified.*

Firstly, imagine this said in a normal tone of voice. Now imagine it this way: beginning in a normal tone, but then getting softer and softer, until you are urgently and slowly whispering, leaving a pause after each phrase. By pausing you increase the tension, and by whispering you recreate the circumstances the protagonist was facing—being as still and silent as possible to avoid agitating the tigers.

Then later, when you talk about springing into action, being chased and escaping, you can speak quickly and loudly to give the impression of action, chaos, panic and ultimately triumph.

Don't use variation in tone just for the sake of it. The way in which you speak should always complement what you are saying. Go through your speech beforehand and work out which bits would be best whispered, which bits would be best shouted, which bits would be best said with passion, and which bits would be best said with cold logic.

Sometimes all this will come naturally, but it can be very helpful to think about it beforehand. And, do you want to leave a long silence somewhere, to allow the audience a moment to think about what you have just said?

Don't be shy. Too many people write speeches about things they care passionately about, and then, because they are afraid of letting rip from the podium, deliver them in an expressionless monotone.

Who do you believe more, a speaker who says 'this is important' in a flat monotone, or someone who shouts the same words while hitting the lectern? The second, right?

If you want your speech to affect people, let it all out. Give a performance.

Feeling the words

Public speakers who insist on presenting a stoic, unemotional face to the world are fighting with one hand behind their backs. Don't be afraid to let emotion into your voice and into yourself when you are public speaking. What you say in any speech or talk should be reinforced by the way in which you say it. If you are explaining the injustice of a particular state of affairs, you will make your point more powerfully if the audience hears the anger in your voice. If you are telling a funny story you should sound as though you are enjoying telling it. When you tell people about something that happened to you, don't just *tell* them—re-live the experience. Let them see how you felt at the time. If you felt sad when your grandfather died, let them see the sadness. If you felt happy when you won the lottery, let them see the joy. If you felt angry when you were sacked, let them see the anger. Almost all good stories involve emotion.

Re-living the emotions associated with your story will make it easier for your audience to live it with you. If you are trying to make an audience care about a cause, for example cancer victims or the homeless, don't be afraid to let yourself feel the story you are telling. Don't just mouth the words. Feel the emotion.

The emotion must, of course, be genuine. Trying to manipulate emotion doesn't work. Simply let yourself experience your own. If you try to do this in a calculated way it will probably backfire—your listeners will see you as insincere. It is far more powerful to express emotion you genuinely feel.

Silences

Learning to use silence effectively can be difficult. Silence scares public speakers. Leaving a pause can feel like a sign of weakness, or of indecision. If you are silent, perhaps the audience will think you've forgotten what you were going to say. 'Quick,' you think, 'fill the space.' Not so fast. A well-timed pause can be enormously effective. Sometimes an audience needs a moment to digest what you have said and to think about it, and a pause gives them that time. Silence can be a powerful tool.

Well-positioned silences can make the audience feel much more involved in your speech. For example, you could say:

> One of the most curious things about the anteater is its remarkable nose. Why is it remarkable? It's remarkable because . . .

Here the technique of asking a question is being used to invite the audience into your speech. But once you ask the question, to effectively allow the audience to become involved you need to give them time to think of the answer. So after you ask 'Why is it remarkable?' leave a pause. And make that pause a bit longer than you think it should be. When you are public speaking, three seconds of silence can feel like three years—but it really is only three seconds, and that's about how long people need to wonder what is remarkable about an anteater's nose.

A pause is also a good way of signalling that something important is coming up. Silence is unusual during a speech, and usually gets everyone's attention immediately. If you've ever been listening to a radio station when a technical problem has cut the broadcast, you may have noticed that at the instant the noise stops everyone stares at the radio. Because the silence is unusual, and has the effect of focusing attention.

Here's how you could talk about the anteater's nose, with pauses:

> And probably the most important thing I want to tell you is this . . .
> (PAUSE—you can sense people leaning in. Now, speaking more softly:)
> one of the most curious things about the anteater is . . .
> (PAUSE—the tension rises: What is it? What is it?)
> its remarkable nose.
> (PAUSE—audience thinks: Its nose? Why its nose?)
> Why is it remarkable?
> (SILENCE—audience is really thinking now)
> (A BIT MORE SILENCE)
> (JUST A BIT MORE)
> It's remarkable because . . .

If you want your audience to be involved in your talk and come on the journey with you, work out before you start when they might need time to think, and give them that time.

Pauses can be also be used to build tension. When the speaker asks why the anteater's nose is remarkable, pausing after the question builds tension. Everyone is wondering what the answer is, and you have their complete attention.

To see a good example of how silence is used to create tension, watch an episode of one of those reality television shows where people are voted off. Even if you don't like the show it's hard not to feel the tension when the host says, 'And the person who has been voted off this week is . . .' and then the host lets the silence hang for 10 or even 20 seconds—which in the age of quick-cut all-action television is a huge amount of time. They do it because they recognise that everyone is hanging out to find out who's leaving. So, sensibly, they milk it.

Ums and ahs

'Um' and 'ah' are two of the most common sounds we make when we're talking, and yet they mean nothing. We use them to give ourselves time to think of what we are going to say next, to buy ourselves a little bit of time to work out how the sentence we've just started will end.

Why don't we just leave silences? We're scared of silence, partly because we're afraid that someone else will jump in and we'll never ever get the chance to finish the sentence.

Umming and ahhing is really irritating. It grates. You may have fantastic content and otherwise be delivering it in a wonderful way, but every um or ah will be sending the message to your audience that you're not sure what comes next, that you lack confidence, that silence scares you. Every meaningless um and ah devalues the rest of your words.

The first step in stopping the habit is to become aware of how much you do it. Ask someone or, if you have the courage, record one of your talks and play it back later, in private. I don't usually advocate this, because it can make you self-conscious and also tempt you to over-analyse your speaking style. The key to public speaking is to be natural. Do the work, and the results will happen. However, because very few of us are aware of our ums and ahs, listening to yourself is a good way to work out whether it is a problem for you.

Just being aware that you um and ah too much will in itself help reduce how often you do it. Try to work out why you are doing it. If it is to buy time, maybe a solution is to be better prepared so that you are certain what is coming up next. Or it may be that you are rushing your whole speech, and need to concentrate on slowing down. When your mouth gets way ahead of your brain, of course you will keep needing to buy time.

Another explanation for umming and ahhing could be nervousness. Using the control strategies I discussed earlier will probably reduce your ums and ahs.

Ask yourself this. If I replace every um and ah with silence, what will happen? Usually your speech will sound more deliberate, more weighted, less rushed and, overall, much better.

The microphone

The first thing to say about microphones is that you should have one. Unless you're speaking to fewer than about 20 people, who are all close to you, you need a microphone. If people have to strain to hear you they are far more likely to lose concentration or become distracted. You want your audience to be able to relax.

If there's a mike stand try to have it adjusted to your height before you go on. You don't want your first 10 seconds on stage to be spent fiddling about. Generally the mike should be about 5 centimetres away from your mouth, but some are strong and some are weak, so check before you start. And remember, if you get too close to it, you'll pop your p's and people will wince.

Don't over-rely on the mike. Some think that having a mike gives them permission to talk like they were sitting next to someone on the bus. It's there to amplify your voice, not to replace its textures. Don't let it interfere with your ability to vary your volume and tone. You can still whisper, you can still shout.

five
PROBLEMS

Something is going wrong. Your talk started great. You connected, you felt them listening to you and you knew they wanted to know what you were going to say next. But now it's getting harder. Why? You thought they loved you, but you can hear them coughing, see them fidgeting, and feel them drifting away. Is it you, you wonder.

Have you suddenly become boring? It's affecting you. The more disengaged the audience seems, the harder it is to talk to them. You're beginning to um and ah, to fidget and you know you're not really connecting with what you are saying anymore, because all you can do is wonder what the heck is going on and what you can do about it. You sneak a look at your watch. Your talk has 20 minutes to go.

What if you're losing them?

How do you know if you're losing the attention of your audience? Sometimes it will be tragically obvious, as when audience members start telling you to 'shut the hell up', or worse. That's happened to me doing stand-up comedy. Feels great. Or they may just start talking to each other. It usually starts from the back, and you have to jump on it quickly because it spreads like a cancer. When people at the back start talking, the people in front of them get distracted. It's harder for them to concentrate on what you are saying, so they start talking too. Then the people in front of them get distracted and start talking, then before you know it you've lost them all.

Why does it happen? Sometimes it's not your fault. Maybe it's been a long day at a conference and people are full up with words, or maybe it's a hot day and there's no airconditioning. Or maybe it is your fault. Maybe your speech started strongly, but you got a bit over-confident and your concentration and commitment dropped. Whatever the reason, if it does happen (and sooner or later it probably will) don't waste time worrying about 'why'. What you need to do is to focus all your energy on getting the audience back.

Don't worry about people yelling abuse at you. Outside the realm of stand-up comedy, it almost never happens. And if it does, there's a section on dealing with hecklers coming up. In most public speaking environments, people won't talk much while you are speaking, apart from whispering asides to the person next to them. That doesn't mean you're not losing them. It just means it's harder for you to work out when you are losing them. If you have ever been in a dull talk or lecture and your mind has drifted away, you have been just as lost to the speaker as if you were yelling abuse. In fact, in some ways you are even more lost, because at least someone yelling abuse is engaging with the speaker. The problem with nice, polite speaking environments is this: if everyone is too respectful to outwardly reveal they are losing interest, then how do you tell if it's happening?

It's kind of tricky. If there's enough light, look at your audience. Some of the signs that you are losing people's attention are crossed arms, being slumped down in the chair, fidgeting, not looking at you, doodling. Sending text messages is a bit of a giveaway too. Listen to them. Lots of coughing, or miscellaneous shuffling noises, means you're probably losing them.

After a while you should be able to sense whether an audience's attention is slipping away. You feel the energy in the room leaking away; the atmosphere dies.

One way of reclaiming attention is to go up a notch in energy. It's amazing how often the injection of a little more oomph into your performance will bring your listeners back. Really concentrate. Speak with passion. Get fired up. Believe what you say. Maybe you started to lose them because your own concentration wandered a bit and you were just going through the motions.

Remember that what you say matters. Speak like what you are saying is the most important thing in the world. Vary your volume. Be as interactive as possible. Pose lots of questions, with pauses to give your audience time to think of an answer. Even ask direct questions if you need to: 'You in the blue shirt in the third row. What do you think is so remarkable about the anteater's nose?' Doing this suddenly changes the dynamic. You give the audience something different and new to watch and listen to. Even if they hate you, they'll still want to know whether the guy in the blue shirt in the third row will manage to come up with a coherent answer or not. And you will have planted the notion in their minds that they could be next. When there's a chance you're going to be asked a question, it suddenly becomes more important to listen.

If you give this tactic a go, do it once and use the added attention you get from it as a springboard. You've asked someone in the audience a question and got everyone's attention. Quick—while you've still got it say something that makes them want to keep listening. Say something important, create some tension, do something in those precious few moments that you have them back to give them a reason to stay with you.

You are dealt about three 'This is important' cards at the start of every speech. That is, if you say to an audience that's slipping away, 'Just listen to this, it's really important', they will probably give you their attention. Their curiosity will be piqued by the fact that you have promised them something important. If you use the second 'card', they will probably listen. And again a third time. But that's usually it. After that, the word 'important' will lose its meaning to them. If you're losing them, play an important card, and then make sure that you say something important.

One of the most effective short-term ways to get an audience to quiet down is to put your mouth close to the microphone and go 'shhhhhh'. It works a treat. If you start the 'shhhhhh' loud and gradually lower its volume, usually the volume of background chatter will lower right along with the volume of your 'shhhhhh'. I don't know why it works so well, but it does. It's almost like having a volume switch. It only works for a few seconds, ten if you're lucky, but again you need to follow up immediately by saying something that gives the audience a reason to want to keep listening.

If you are speaking to a noisy room, especially when you are an MC and have to keep hopping up and down all night, nothing works as well as hitting a glass with a fork in front of the micro-phone. It is much more dignified then standing up there saying, 'Excuse me . . . hello . . . can I just have everyone's attention for a moment? . . . hi . . .' etc.

Two of the scariest ways of trying to pull an audience back are talking more softly and using silence. When you feel an audience slipping away, especially if they are starting to talk, your instinct is to talk louder and faster. That rarely works. But if you stop talking, you will usually get everyone's attention, if only for the reason that they want to know whether you've had a breakdown on stage. Speakers speak, so when you stop speaking, they want to know why. So a long pause can actually focus attention.

If you start speaking softer and softer, suddenly the people up the back talking among themselves won't be able to hear you. Now it's all very well to ignore someone when you can hear them, but when they can't hear you, suddenly they want to know what they are missing. How can you ignore someone properly when you can't even hear them? Often if you start speaking softer everyone will lean in to catch what you are saying.

All of these are techniques I have seen work. None of them guarantees success. Sometimes you are going to lose an audience no matter what. If you do a lot of public speaking, it's inevitable. And you learn much more from those gigs than you do from the ones that go well.

If it's going downhill and nothing seems to be able to drag it back, you may prefer to cut your losses, edit your speech heavily on the run, wrap it up and get off. That's often the best thing to do. It's the best thing to do in terms of your self-esteem, and if the audience doesn't like you being on they will be grateful that you cut it short. On the other hand, if you have been engaged to provide a particular service, or to speak for a particular time, you need to consider the impact that cutting and running will have.

Could it mean that you don't get paid? Sometimes the fact that the audience is disengaged is part of the gig. (If teachers or lecturers cut and ran whenever they felt they were losing an audience, a lot of classes would be over in ten minutes.)

Heckling

It's all very well to deliver a speech to an audience that is willing to receive it. But how do you cope with being heckled?

I define heckling as anything that interrupts the speaker or distracts members of the audience. So yes, heckling can be someone shouting 'piss off', but it can also be a cough, a noisy airconditioner, or a mobile phone. I have been heckled by all of them, as well as by mirror balls, the wind, faulty microphones, kitchens, cappuccino machines and a dog.

In my view the speaker *should* respond to anything that distracts the audience, because it shows they are in control of their environment and it builds the respect of the audience. A respectful audience is a good audience.

In addition, it is *essential* that a speaker respond to anything that threatens their authority over the audience; that is, anything that deliberately or thoughtlessly distracts the audience.

The first thing to do when you're heckled is to assess the threat. Ask yourself whether the heckle is going to distract a fair number of the audience. If someone coughs once, no. If someone is persistently coughing their lungs up, perhaps then the answer is yes. (Probably the best thing to do there is to simply ask the person if they're all right, and politely suggest they may want to go and get a glass of water. That way you are being nice, but also making it clear it is a distraction. They probably feel bad about interrupting you.) If something distracts a significant proportion of the audience, you should respond.

Work out how big an interruption the heckle is. Is it a one-off, or is it likely to be repeated? Was it a deliberate attempt to unsettle you or distract the audience, or just an accident? If, for example, a loud car alarm is clearly audible for a few moments, then yes, it has distracted the audience, but no, it's not likely to be repeated (although it could be), and no, it was not a deliberate attempt to unsettle you. You could get away without acknowledging it and just move on. However, it is something that has intruded upon your talk and distracted people, so ideally you should acknowledge it in some way—perhaps: 'That's someone stealing my car but I don't care because talking to you is more important'.

What if a mobile phone rings while you are talking? It happens all the time. If it's turned off quickly, you can get away with ignoring it. Again, however, most of the audience will probably have been distracted by it so you should say something. 'If it's for me tell them I'm busy. In fact if it's for you, tell them you're busy', for example.

What if a mobile rings during your talk and the person answers it? It happens. It's a big interruption, it's hopefully a one-off, but if it's not a deliberate attempt to sabotage you, then it's at least very thoughtless (unless of course the person is a heart surgeon on call). If you don't acknowledge and deal with what amounts to a blatant threat to your authority, the audience's respect for you will go downhill fast. They will be thinking what you are thinking: that the person who's answered their phone is rude and should be put in their place. The only person who can do that is you. If you don't, you will have failed the audience.

In this situation, you don't need to be witty. All you need to do is to voice the thoughts of the audience. For example: 'Did you just answer your phone in the middle of my speech? I think that's one of the rudest things I've ever seen. Does anyone agree?' Don't say it with anger though. Anger suggests you are losing control, and you don't want the audience to think that.

When it comes to dealing with interruptions, public speakers have a huge advantage over most other performers. We can acknowledge the distraction and respond to it, whereas actors in a play, for example, are trapped by their script. If a mobile phone rings in their audience they can't do a thing about it.

The worst thing you can do is to ignore a heckle. A distraction will remain a distraction until you deal with it. And if you don't, everyone in the audience will wonder why, and because they are wondering why, they will lose focus, drift away, lose respect for you. Generally, the bigger the distraction, and the more it is deliberately, even thoughtlessly, aimed at you, the more respect you will lose if you fail to deal with it.

Some distractions, like a loud airconditioner or overflowing noise from elsewhere, you can do nothing about. But you should still acknowledge them. Again, your response doesn't necessarily have to be witty or clever. It can be enough to say, 'I'm sorry we've got all that noise from next door. Apparently it's a wedding reception. There's nothing we can do about it, so I'll speak up and please bear with me.' At least you have acknowledged the problem, explained what it is, told them that we're all in this together and asked for their help. The alternative, not mentioning it, will just mean that all through your talk people will be distracted, thinking, 'Gee it's hard to concentrate with that noise. I wonder what it is. Isn't there something they can do about it? Why hasn't the speaker mentioned it? Can't she hear it?'

When you respond to a distraction, part of what you are doing is verbalising the audience's irritation. By being their voice in letting off steam, a problem shared becomes a problem halved, as you and your audience band together against the common enemy, the distraction.

The best responses to hecklers are funny. But when you respond quickly, spontaneously and in a way that is clearly improvised, what you say doesn't have to be all that funny to get a laugh. In fact, if you can say anything halfway decent your audience will give you a great reaction. There are two reasons for this. One is that they'll be enormously impressed that you managed to think of something even mildly witty right off the top of your head. The other is that everyone there really wants you to beat the heckler. Whether it's an airconditioner or a drunk, they are desperately hoping you'll win—because if you do you will have proved you are worth listening to, and they will feel they have made the right decision in coming to hear you speak. You were tested and you passed. But if you can't respond, it means they're stuck listening to a loser. And they don't want that. In their heads they are saying, 'Please, please, please say something halfway decent, so we can all breathe a sigh of relief and go with you.'

Give them half a reason to side with you and they will. The same psychology lies behind the fact that the more an audience pays to see you, the more positively they will react. If they have paid two dollars they don't really care if you are any good. It's only two bucks. But if they have paid forty bucks, they really want you to be good, and they will do everything they can to ensure that you are good—because if you aren't, they've done their money.

How do you respond in a witty way to heckling? Look hard, listen hard and be open to things. If there's a lot of noise from the room next door, maybe there's been something in the news that will help. Perhaps someone famous is visiting town or getting married—and you can joke that it's them. If a coffee machine keeps interrupting you, talk to it like it's a person. Make up a reason why it's giving you a hard time (it saw you with a cup of tea earlier and it got jealous).

If the distraction is not deliberately aimed at you (a coughing fit, a crying baby), don't show anger. You can show frustration and exasperation but do it with a smile. Keeping your good humour in difficult circumstances will win you respect.

A person who is treating you with disrespect needs to be treated firmly. Hit the heckling on the head early and show who's boss. The audience wants you to deal with the situation, to show that you are the boss, because they want to be spared the embarrassment of the opposite being proven true. If you can come up with something adequate, they will give you the benefit of the doubt and go with you.

The easiest human hecklers to deal with are the isolated ones. For example, one person with a mobile phone, or a couple of people talking when everyone else wants to listen, or one person shouting out something that is neither clever nor funny. In these cases, everyone else in the audience wants them to shut up. Ideally, the speaker should express, preferably in a light and funny way, the hostility and irritation the audience are feeling toward the heckler. Or you can do it directly: 'Excuse me can you be quiet.' If the heckler says something that is clearly intended to be funny but isn't, then an easy response for the speaker is to make it clear that it wasn't funny. For example: 'You thought that was going to be funny, didn't you? Guess what? You were wrong.' If the heckler says something nonsensical, an effective response is often to repeat what was said, puzzle over it and examine it, all the while reinforcing to the audience just how silly it actually was.

You don't have to stamp on every human heckler. A common mistake is to treat every interjection as a threat. Sometimes, especially in small crowds, a person will say something just because they are feeling relaxed, it's a nice vibe and they want to join in. Their intention isn't to threaten you, but to add something to the discussion. You may ask a rhetorical question you don't expect to be answered, and someone jumps in with an answer. If that person is not motivated by drunken idiocy, but rather is genuinely trying to add something, their interjection should be treated with respect. (In fact, it is a compliment to you that you have managed to relax an audience member to such an extent that they have added a comment.) The worst thing you can do in this situation is to get scared and defensive and verbally jump on the interjector. It makes you look mean and will immediately alienate the audience. The heckler wasn't trying to do any harm and he got hammered for no reason. The audience will think you were unfair, and they'll be right.

The reason for over-reacting in this situation is insecurity. Rather than listening to the content of what's said and the tone in which it's said, all we register is that there has been an interruption. We get scared of losing control and immediately go into attack mode. If someone is just trying to join in without malice, you need to spot that and react accordingly. Take on board what the person has said and see where it goes. If it's stupid, you can point that out in a gentle way and you can all have a laugh. But if it's a good suggestion, explore it and see what happens. Never dish out more to a heckler than they deserve.

There is a law of proportionality. When someone heckles cruelly they give a speaker licence to go at them as long and hard as he wishes. The audience understands the heckler started it and even if it turns out to be as uneven a conflict as, say, Luxembourg versus the USA, they will remember that Luxembourg started it. But if the comment was merely an attempt—perhaps misguided—to be interesting or funny rather than malicious, the audience may accept a quick putdown, but too hard or prolonged a counterattack will transfer their sympathy to the heckler. If that happens, then it's a long way back for the speaker.

If you find that you have overstepped the mark and verbally hit someone harder than they deserve, the best thing is to admit you've made a mistake and apologise.

If someone is really going at you, however, then the gloves come off. An aggressive heckler is dangerous and must be dealt with firmly and quickly. The alternative is humiliation. Usually the only place that aggressive personal heckling occurs is at stand-up gigs, and then usually only on Friday or Saturday nights when too much alcohol has been consumed. Then it can get aggressive, personal and crude. Most comedians work out a couple of standard lines that they can use as a response to a personal attack. They imagine some drunk bloke (hecklers are very rarely women) shouting 'piss off', 'you're not funny' or 'you've got a big nose' (I've had all these) and write a couple of witty responses. If you are not going to do stand-up comedy you don't need to worry about this type of heckling.

The most dangerous form of heckling is the widespread and low-level sort that arises when people lose interest and begin to talk among themselves, as discussed in the previous section. When you see that two or more people have disengaged from what you are saying and are talking amongst themselves you need to do something fast. If you can hear them, other people can too. You can try and engage with the talkers, ask them what they are talking about. They can't ignore you when they are being directly addressed and that will at least bring them back into the fold. Or you can politely and reasonably say that you don't mind if they talk, but other people are trying to listen. Then give them the choice to stay or go:

I don't want you to stay unless you want to listen, and I suspect no one else does either, so it's totally up to you.

Stay or go. But if you want to keep talking you may as well go.

Then give them a moment to leave. If they leave that's good. If they don't, then they have implicitly agreed to shut up, and if they don't shut up the audience will be angry, thus giving you permission to be forceful and rude to them. They may even, if you ask them to, all turn around and as one go 'shhhhhh' to the talkers.

If you confront difficult situations like this head on, you'll win brownie points from your audience.

Every heckler is a challenge and an opportunity. If you can deal with the heckler you will have shown the audience that you're worth listening to and that you deserve respect. It's scary, but if you're in the moment you'll often surprise yourself with your ability to say just the right thing.

Booze

It's often been said that a boozed-up audience is a speaker's friend, especially a speaker who's trying to be funny. That's sort of right and sort of wrong. Yes, a couple of drinks does help audience members to relax and get them laughing more easily. For three reasons, I think. One, add a glass or two of alcohol to a person and they will usually find pretty much everything a bit funnier. Two, people are less self-conscious when they're been drinking and so worry less about whether everyone else will laugh and how silly they will look if they are the only one. And three, after a bit of alcohol every noise a person makes, including laughter, gets louder.

Booze can just as easily become the speaker's enemy, however. People who have drunk too much find it harder to follow what you are saying, their concentration span diminishes, their IQ lowers, and they are more inclined to interrupt. Being less self-conscious, they will heckle more and talk to their friends more. And they will talk loudly, quite unaware of what a distraction it is for you and the rest of the audience.

If you end up with an audience full of drunks, one way to appeal to them is to take out anything clever and substitute swear words. Audiences full of people who are very drunk usually find swear words very, very funny. I don't know why.

Generally, at an evening function that starts about 7 p.m., the time by which people have had enough to drink so that they are relaxed, but not so much as to be difficult, is between 8 and 10 p.m. I don't advise going on any later than 10 p.m.

If you walk around the room you'll be able to sense how much people have been drinking, and whether it's too late or not. You can usually get a fair idea just from the level of noise. The louder the conversation, the more booze has been consumed.

What about alcohol for the speaker? Many a time I've heard people who are about to make a speech say, 'I'll just have a couple of drinks and I'll be right.' Beware. Yes, alcohol does disinhibit and relax, and if you are nervous those can be attractive qualities. However, alcohol can also affect your judgment and your speed of thought, and make you slur your speech—none of which is good. I used to never drink before I went on. Now I'm a bit more relaxed about it. If I'm speaking after dinner, I might have a glasses or two of wine with dinner. I can do that without it having any negative effect.

six

DIFFERENT TYPES OF SPEECHES

The boss speaks

How should a boss talk to his or her staff? Speeches by bosses are given hundreds of times a day, ranging from the head of a big company speaking at an end-of-year dinner to a section head addressing a group at a weekly staff meeting.

If you are the boss or, to put it in modern jargon, if the people you are talking to 'report to you', they will usually listen very carefully to what you say and analyse it afterwards. They will do this because what you say and think and do affects them.

Speeches given by a boss have higher stakes than most other speeches. Usually, when audiences don't like what they're hearing, they switch off and when the speech is over they never think about it again. But if you are the boss, they can't do that. The effects of a bad speech will linger. If those who report to you have been bored or alienated or irritated by what you have said, that impression will affect how they react to you in the future and their motivation to work for the organisation.

People want a boss who cares. They want to feel needed and appreciated. They hate to be taken for granted. If they like what they hear from their boss, if they are inspired by it, they will be happier, more motivated and more productive. Every time a boss speaks, therefore, it is a chance to motivate.

There are, broadly speaking, two ways of motivating people: the carrot and the stick or, to put it another way, inspiration and fear. In speaking to a group of people who report to you, the carrot is far more effective than the stick.

I believe that pretty much every speech made by a boss should contain some variation of this core message:

> *You are important. We need you. We're all in this together. Thank you for all your hard work. Without you this company wouldn't work. I know it's hard. Together I believe we can do even better. New and exciting challenges await. Good luck. Once again thank you.*

The aim of such a speech is simple: to have people at the end of it think, 'I'm valued, I'm needed, I'm challenged, I want to succeed, let's go!'

So if you are giving a training seminar on how to sell your company's new washing machine, for example, don't get bogged down in the technical data. The most important thing you can say to your staff is:

You are the people who actually sell our product and without you this company wouldn't exist. I know it's hard work and I want to thank you. With this new product I think we can do even better. I hope you do too and you want to take up that challenge.

Try to instil in them a feeling of belonging and of ownership. The more they feel like they are part of an organisation, rather than just an employee of it, the more motivated they will be.

A boss shouldn't waste words. Keep what you say special. If there is a lot of technical or organisational information to be covered, think about other ways you can do it. Email, printed material, someone else speaking . . . Make your words count, and ensure that if you are speaking to people you only get to speak to occasionally that they get the core message: that they are important and appreciated. If you are telling them about the future of the company, remember that what they most want to know is what it means for them. It's all very well to talk about the company's plans to expand and increase market share, but you will not connect unless you explain to your staff what that means for them. Does it mean an increase in wages, or just more work? Does it mean better conditions, or just higher profits for others? Everyone who goes to work has at least one reason for doing so, and that is to get paid. When you speak to those who report to you, try to give them another reason to come to work; give them a sense of shared challenge, or set them a goal they may feel excited to try to achieve, or try to inspire in them a belief in the importance of their work.

The role of the MC

The role of an MC or compere can be tricky, but it's important. The MC sets the tone for an evening or event and is responsible for ensuring that things run smoothly. The most important part is making a good start. If you start well and people like you, then every time you return they will think, 'Ah, here's that person we like again.' If you start badly, each time you come on again they will inwardly groan.

Give yourself every advantage you can. MCs don't usually get introduced. It's their job to introduce everyone else. But don't wander up on stage unannounced if you can help it. Try to get hold of an off-stage microphone and ask someone to announce you. Or do it yourself. (Then when you go on you can make a joke about how you had to introduce yourself.) Make the announcement about ten seconds long, as it can take that long to gather everyone's attention. So say it slowly and put in some extra words. For example:

> *Ladies and gentlemen, welcome to the 2006 Excellence in Woodchopping Awards. Please welcome to the stage your master of ceremonies for this evening . . .*

Have a glass and a fork stashed near the mike so you can tap one onto the other in front of it if there is still chatter when you go on. Then start strong. Be fluent, welcoming, and ideally a little bit funny. Tell them why the function you're at is going to be great, but don't run through what's going to happen in too much detail. MCs often have to do lots of 'housekeeping', that is, telling everyone where the toilets are or why they should buy raffle tickets or where lunch is going to be served or finding out who owns the car that still has its headlights on. Try not to do this right

DIFFERENT TYPES OF SPEECHES

at the start because it sends a message you are going to be dull. Also, don't blather on for too long at the start, unless you're being really entertaining, because that will send the message to the audience that you're a blatherer. Do a few minutes of light, engaging, slightly funny stuff then get off and that will set you up for the rest of the event.

Often you can do the necessary housekeeping in a light way, with lots of humour thrown in, but the most important thing is to get through this information as quickly and efficiently as possible. Send a message that you are not going to talk just for the sake of it. Let the audience know that you respect the fact that they are listening to you, and you are not going to abuse that privilege.

When an MC introduces another speaker, their most important role is to deliver that speaker an attentive audience. Sometimes that means taking a bullet yourself. If the audience is not attentive to you, the temptation is to get out of there quickly by introducing the speaker immediately. That's a big no-no. You need to get the audience's attention before you hand over, which might mean you have to stand up there for a while and try to settle them.

Make your introductions crisp and brief. Have a chat to the person you are going to introduce beforehand and if there's nothing obvious, ask if there's anything in particular they want you to say to introduce them. Usually they'll say 'no', but it's nice to ask. Try to get some information on them before the day and pick out a couple of the most relevant and interesting things. Two or three sentences is usually enough. There's rarely a good reason for an intro to be longer than that. (See Being Introduced on page 113.)

If the audience is proving difficult to settle, make the person you are introducing sound important, build them up to create

163

interest. You may even have to say, 'You should listen to this, it'll be very interesting'. Or you can, schoolteacher-like, ask the audience to show some politeness and respect for the guest speaker.

It's important for an MC to listen to what's happening when they're not on stage, so that when you go back on you are able to comment on what the speaker has been talking about. Ideally you should be able to say something funny about it. There will usually be something in what they've said that you can grab hold of.

You will often notice when you come back on after a speaker that there is a rise in background noise from the audience. This is because the MC inevitably tends to become part of the background (the audience knows who you are, and they naturally relax after the guest speaker has finished and chat about whether the speaker was any good or not). There's not much you can do about it. Get used to it. It's not your fault.

At the end of the night finish off quickly. Don't summarise—the audience knows what has happened. You may want to tell a short story that sums up something you are going to take away from the function, just as if you were ending a speech (see The End on page 86). Otherwise, just wrap it up, thank anyone who should be thanked, tell them you hope they've enjoyed it, say thank you and get off.

Motivating generosity: speaking at fundraisers

If you are speaking at a function where the purpose is to raise money for a charity or some other cause, there are some specific things to remember.

It is even more important than normal to keep the audience happy, because a happy audience is more likely to be generous.

Some charity functions are so full of speeches, auctions, raffle draws and thank yous that the audience has no chance to talk and have fun. People who have time to talk will be more generous. Auctions are a great way of raising money, but limit the amount of auction items to less than ten, ideally five or six, and do the rest by silent auction. Have the main fundraising activity, usually the auction, after the main meal, after the intake of alcohol has loosened not only tongues but wallets.

It is important that you precede the main fundraising activity with a speech that motivates people to give, which I believe is a speech that includes the following:

1. Identify the cause money is being raised for. For example, 'All money raised tonight will go towards research into finding a cure for cancer'.

2. Explain how big a problem it is in language people will understand and make it clear how it's relevant to those in the audience. For example, 'Two out of every seven people will be directly affected by cancer before they turn 75. There are 210 people here tonight, so that means 60 of us.'

3. Get the audience to identify with the cause by asking them to imagine they are directly affected. If the function is to raise money for the blind: 'Imagine not being able to see. Imagine how many things you take for granted that you'd be unable to do. Shut your eyes now. Imagine if it was like that all the time.' Get them to stand in the shoes of a person who is blind. Tell a story about a person who is blind, or, even better, get that person to tell their own story.

4. Tell your audience how the money raised will be used to make a real difference to people's lives. For example, 'Every dollar raised tonight will go directly to providing services that assist people without sight.'

5. Ask them to be generous.

Job interviews

You might not think of a job interview as public speaking, but if you think of the person or persons interviewing you as an audience, then what is required to deliver a successful job interview is very similar to what is required to give a successful speech. In a job interview you are trying to win over an audience (of one or more) to the belief that you are the best person for the job. All the things that are important in public speaking—preparation, confidence, presentation and so on—are important in a job interview too.

Of course you can't write a speech because you don't know what questions you will be asked, right? Wrong. If you think about it, you can usually work out what many of the areas they will cover are going to be. Write out answers to likely questions. Practise saying them.

Before the interview, employ the techniques I've suggested for controlling your nervousness. During the interview, use the same presentation methods as you do when public speaking. Engage with the interviewers, make vigorous eye contact, look alive and enthusiastic. Don't let your words leak unconvincingly out of your mouth, fill the room with them. Be serious where you need to be, passionate where you can be, and humorous if it's appropriate. Your interviewers are your audience and they need to be won over. Don't be put off by a lack of response, but use all your skills to reach out to them and win them. At the same time, don't overdo things to the extent that you seem overbearing or pushy.

When making a presentation to a client or a boss, bear the same things in mind. Prepare thoroughly, anticipate likely questions and practise answers, control your nerves and present in an engaged, enthusiastic and confident way.

Ad-libbing

People find the idea of ad-libbing on stage terrifying. What they forget is that every single one of us is an expert at ad-libbing. Every single conversation you have ever had has been ad-libbed. There was no script, you just made it up as you went along. Every time we have a conversation our minds have to work incredibly fast, they have to make hundreds of decisions every minute. You have to listen to what others are saying and then work out how to respond. You have to pick the words you want to respond with and use them in the right order. As you begin a sentence, you have to work out what the sentence is about, where it is going, and how it will end. You need to work out when to stop talking and let the other person have a go. Should you end with a question or is it obvious from what you have said where the conversation will head next? It's actually incredibly complicated and yet we all do it successfully dozens of times every day.

But, you might think, giving a speech is harder. In a conversation you are continually prompted and stimulated by what the other person says. Yes, but look at it this way. Whenever you say something in conversation that goes for more than about 20 seconds, you are giving a completely ad-libbed short speech. If you tell any type of story about what you did that day, or talk about your political or religious beliefs, or proffer an opinion about a story in the news, you are ordering and delivering your thoughts in the same way as when you give a speech.

In other words, ad-libbing is not an alien technique to any of us. If we want to ad lib on stage, it is not a new skill we need to learn. It is a skill we already have. We just need to learn how to use it somewhere new, that is, on stage. Learning to ad lib on stage is not like a novice learning to play the violin. It's more like already knowing how to play the violin, but having to learn how to do it while simultaneously riding a bicycle.

To prove to yourself that you are capable of ad-libbing a speech, do this. Right now, in your head, give a one-minute speech on the subject of flowers. Go!

What happened? Did you freeze, unable to think of anything, or fly into a blind panic? I bet you didn't. I bet you just said a few of the things that immediately came into your head when you thought about flowers. Congratulations. You just ad-libbed a speech.

We can all ad lib in conversation because we are relaxed and we're not self-conscious about it. If we kept thinking about it how hard it actually is, it would be a lot more difficult. We need to transfer the relaxed way in which we ad lib in everyday life onto the stage.

But, you might say, do I really need to be able to ad lib on stage? If I can write and deliver a good speech, isn't that enough? If you want to be the best public speaker you can be, you need to have the full arsenal of weapons available, and one of them is the ability to think on your feet and speak spontaneously. You will need to do that when you answer questions from the audience, and when you deal with interruptions and hecklers. If you realise five minutes into a speech that it is not working because you have pitched it wrongly, if you can ad lib you will be able to adjust what you are saying on the run. More importantly, the knowledge that you are capable of speaking confidently off the cuff will give you far greater self-confidence on stage.

Practice is the key. When I started regularly speaking in public, I used to lie in bed before I went to sleep and make myself deliver a couple of silent speeches on random topics. The more you practise making stuff up on the spot the better you'll get at it. When you are giving a speech to a small audience and the stakes aren't high, take a risk. Ad lib. Follow tangents. See what happens. Look at your script less and less and trust that you know what you are talking about. Just talk. If it doesn't work, go back to your script. Take up all opportunities for taking questions from the floor. That will give you experience at speaking spontaneously.

The other thing to do is to try, when you are on stage, to get into the relaxed state of mind you are in when you're taking part in everyday conversation. Once again, this comes back to being in the moment. If you keep working on controlling your nerves and being utterly present on stage, you will be far better able to react to what happens right now, and speak honestly and articulately off the top of your head.

The big finish

You may be able to learn the theory of changing a car tyre by listening to someone talk about it, but ultimately you won't know whether you can actually do it until you have a go and get your hands dirty. Public speaking is the same. Some people talk about how they want to make speeches or do stand-up comedy for years but never actually do it. They fear failure. We all do. But I fear something else even more—regret—getting to the end of my life and wishing I had had the guts to have a go at something.

Just as very few people are good at playing the violin the first time they do it, very few people are good at public speaking the first time they do it. I wasn't. So don't expect too much too soon. While at one level public speaking is very simple—all it involves is talking to people—it is also very complicated. There is a lot to remember, and then you have to forget it all and just do it. Very few good public speakers, while on stage, actually think consciously about any of the things I have discussed. They just do it. But it's there underneath. It becomes instinct.

The more you do it the better you will be at it. There is a saying in stand-up comedy: 'You have to die before you can live'. It means that before you can get the satisfaction and joy that comes with doing great gigs, you have to go through the unpleasant and gruelling process of doing bad gigs. It is from those bad gigs, where you feel the audience slipping away and yourself becoming disconnected from your own words, that you learn the most. It feels terrible but it prompts you to get better.

It is impossible to judge whether you can be a good speaker or not from one or two speeches, just as it is impossible to tell after one lesson whether you will be a good violin player. Keep doing it. I have seen new comedians battle through months and months of hardly getting a laugh and then suddenly, as if by magic, they get it right. Usually you can't really tell what is different. Somehow the person had found herself or himself on stage. Keep doing it and it will probably happen.

For me, public speaking is one of the most rewarding things I have ever done. It has increased my self-confidence immeasurably. It feels fantastic to have a whole room of people silent and expectant, all waiting with baited breath to hear what you will say next.

I hope you do it enough to enjoy it as much as I have. Good luck.